THE WANDERING LIFE

FOLLOWED BY

ANOTHER ERA OF WRITING

THE FRENCH LIST

YVES BONNEFOY

The Wandering Life

FOLLOWED BY

Another Era of Writing

TRANSLATED AND WITH AN AFTERWORD

BY HOYT ROGERS

LONDON NEW YORK CALCUTTA

PAP
TAGORE

The work is published with the support of the
Publication Assistance Programmes of the Institut français

Seagull Books, 2023

'*The Wandering Life*' *followed by* '*Another Era of Writing*' was first
published as '*La Vie errante*' *suivi de* '*Une autre époque de l'écriture*'
© Mercure de France, 1993

First published in English translation by Seagull Books, 2023
English translation and Afterword © Hoyt Rogers, 2023

ISBN 978 1 80309 240 9

British Library Cataloguing-in-Publication Data
A catalogue record for this book is available from the British Library

Typeset by Seagull Books, Calcutta, India
Printed and bound by Hyam Enterprises, Calcutta, India

CONTENTS

The Wandering Life   1

'READ THE BOOK!'   3

THE WANDERING LIFE   11

    The Colour Alchemist   13

    The Wandering Life   18

    All Morning in the City   20

    The Northern Fire   25

    Strabo the Geographer   27

    Glaucus the God   28

    As Far as I Know You   29

    The Clock   30

    Sugarfoot   31

    Impressions at Sunset   33

    Huge Red Rocks   35

    Landscape with the Flight into Egypt   40

    All the Gold in the World   43

THE GRAPES OF ZEUXIS   45

    The Grapes of Zeuxis   47

    The Dogs   48

    The Top of the World   49

    Night   50

    The Task of Non-Existence   51

    The Blind Man   52

    The Incision   53

    The Book   54

    They Spoke to Me   55

THE GRAPES OF ZEUXIS AGAIN   57

    Incompletable   59

    The Painter's Despair   60

    The Museum   61

    Nocturnal Justice   62

    Homage   63

    The Great Image   64

    The Crucifix   65

    The Grapes of Zeuxis Again   66

    She Who Invented Painting   68

LAST GRAPES OF ZEUXIS   69

    I.   *Zeuxis, despite the birds*   71

    II.   *He caught his breath*   72

    III.   *And what a surprise it was*   73

    IV.   *Not even those weighty clusters*   74

    V.   *Now, he paints in peace*   75

    VI.   *Long, long hours*   76

    VII.   *Ah, what's happened?*   77

    VIII.   *Zeuxis wanders in the countryside*   78

    IX.   *It's something akin to a puddle*   79

FROM WIND AND SMOKE   81

A STONE   91

TWO MUSICIANS, THREE PERHAPS   95

    Two Musicians, Three Perhaps   97

    Three Memories of the Journey   100

    Two Sentences, and Others   103

    Hands That Take Hold of His   106

    Zeuxis: The Self-Portrait   108

BECKETT'S DINGHY   111

Another Era of Writing 119

Bonnefoy the Voyager: A Translator's Afterword 151

Translator's Acknowledgements 169

The Wandering Life

'READ THE BOOK!'

The garden was full of orange-trees; their shadows were blue, and birds cheeped in their branches. A large vessel, all its lights ablaze, slowly advanced between silent river-banks. What is colour? he wondered. He'd just opened the small, low gate; its wood was crumbling, shearing off in flakes after so many years, so many rains. Perhaps colour is the sign God makes to us the whole world over: this green, this blue, or this reddish ochre is like a sentence that makes no sense and so comes to a halt . . . like the boat? It had stopped. All the people going to and fro on one of its bridges became more visible now: black silhouettes over little tongues of fire, surrounded by smoke. But the world has no colours, as we so naively believe, he said to himself again. Only colour exists, and its shadows, whether places or things, are merely its way of cleaving to itself alone, looking out for itself, seeking a shore. Night falls, day breaks, but it's always the same blue, sometimes grey, or the same red throughout the hours, isn't it? And as to words! —Already they were disembarking: children, many children who ran in every direction, laughing; then an elderly woman, her head encircled by flames; then an old man leaning on a young man's arm, dressed in white. And so many others as well! But he who was also arriving no longer looked at them; pensively, he walked along in the orange-grove, on the sand.

As to words! Who has claimed that they're only a faulty evocation of things, because their sounds—their colours—might add their resonance to the world? The word night is bright, but so is the night itself, just as much as it is dark. Or rather night is neither bright nor dark, it's simply a word, like the fallen orange or the bluish grass. Still meditating, now he treaded on that grass between the trees. He sat down among them, since his fatigue had grown after crossing the garden's threshold, with all the heat of summer streets on the nape of his neck. A tall black woman has come to lean her elbows on the windowsill, next to her son. Without a word, they both watch the falling night, or else the rising sun, a bit of very sombre red above the port: it's deserted on that side of the quays, and even covered up by big stones.

Tomorrow the boat will leave again, with them on board; or else it will stay there, rusting. And they themselves disembarked from it yesterday—or when? They're walking now, almost randomly, on the sand. I know you well, he'd said to the little girl dressed in red, when he was still only a child. I know you, I recognize you. You were coming towards me for such a long time with these palm fronds in your hands—it was the sky, wasn't it? You were very small, and behind you was pure colour, its high waves tilting against the jetty of time, swirling without a sound.

He strolls further into the garden. From now on, there are wide pathways everywhere: far off, their arches of leaves and fruits narrow onto a blue shadow of mosaics, or perhaps a canvas that glints. But this trail he wanted to follow, then another one soon after, then more of them still . . . they all fork quickly on powdery sand where his footsteps sink, as if on a sloping dune. The oranges are ripe: plentiful and heavy, in their bottomless basket of low branches. Here's a bench, and he sits down; he lays a book beside him he doesn't plan to read. The mother and son face the night; the fire behind them glows on two raised stones, in the darkened room. The starry sky spreads beneath their feet, into the infinite—its dazzling clusters bereft of any rays, any gleams in the inky blackness.

How peaceful everything is around this bench, as he leans against the trunk of an ancient tree . . . as the heat stiches embroideries, almost transparent, in the fabric of bluish grass. How good it is to live amid the somnolence of the world: a massive nude who stirs at times without waking—hair scattered against the sheets, zebraed with light and shade by the blinds . . . He listens to that even breathing. He sits up a bit. He takes this hand, unaware of itself, and loosens its unresisting fingers one by one, as they shed a hint of the dream, no doubt.

But what's this he's been hearing now for a while? This monotonous noise, like the tireless, annoying dings he used to make, in the tiny garden of his childhood? With his little rake, he'd strike an iron bucket, sometimes filled to the brim with moist dirt. Three dings, then a pause, then three or four more, then again, the mystery of silence— repeating on and on for the longest time, although he didn't want to! He feared they'd rush from up there to shout that they'd had enough; but no one called out, no one hastened down to him from those high stairs . . . And so he had to walk on beneath all these skies, forever alone.

'Read the book!' Suddenly he's understood that these are the words, and that the sounds he was hearing, that he listens to now, are the words of a child who's softly singing, who's pretending to chant. He's all alone, no doubt, in the sunroom of a nearby house. A small boy in a wicker chair, he sways while holding a picture book in his hands—a book from which colour leaks out.

And the man jumps up: he's already striding straight through the trees as they melt before him. He comes across another gate—a low, faded barrier as well—which opens onto the other garden. He follows its short path of old, beaten earth, then climbs the stairs. The child has fallen silent. He's poring over the book. He's placed it in front of him on a little table—where there are pencil crayons, too, along with brushes and vials of bright paints. And he who's just arrived moves closer still. 'I'll take your small face in my hands, my God. I'll turn it towards me, gently. I'll tell you: Open your eyes again. Forgive me for having wandered on the earth.'

But no, not at all: he hasn't left the bench under the orange-trees, and his own book is nothing more than a notebook of thick grey paper, or yellowish brown. It's stitched with twine, like those that beginners learnt to draw in long ago. For him, certainly—for a child—the drawings would be of large, simple things and beings and animals; with them he'd been told he'd have to live one day, awkwardly—and also die. The orange in the orange-tree; the boat that glides forward among the branches; the beautiful figure—this woman—upright in black at the prow; and the dog, the cat, the cat's bowl of milk the dog knocks over; the mouse that runs; the little boy, the little girl. And certain words—if they're words these shadows that shift; and certain sentences—if they're sentences these cries of sudden recognition, these embraces, these hands that join as if forever, these statues with eyes shut, these enormous clouds over there, red because the sun has already started to set. Read the book—what book?

Now he believes that the voice has fallen silent; that the sunroom over there is empty—like the garden all around him, like the white roads further still, like the world. He believes that there is nothing in the world but colour: meant to fade away, to trickle into the sand. All the same, he hopes and dreams that a hand unknown to him will gently open his fingers one by one; will place a coloured pencil into them, then close them again—yet without saying anything, and with no one coming from inside the house to help him create the world.

THE WANDERING LIFE

The Colour Alchemist

He was convinced that just as we can produce gold from the most ordinary metals, we can also transmute colours—those minerals of the mind—into gold's equivalent: the light.

So he set to work. He mixed the most varied colours, but all he ever got was grey: that mud they formed on the good-sized board, quite smooth, he'd chosen for his experiments. Days, then years of research! The most singular names, borrowed from Pythagoras, from the Platonists, from the Cabalists, yielded the batches of blue or red which he proposed to green, to saffron yellow, to indigo. But all in vain. He ground the rarest earth minerals, and the coarsest as well. The purest waters—but also the murkiest at times, where iridescent glints fleet by like dreams. These cleansed his mistakes, and countered his despairs. But in vain, always in vain. No matter how much the colours on wooden palettes met each other and interfused; no matter how much even the most delicate brushes—for lining the edges of eyelids, for deepening the gaze—melded the hues as patiently, as inwardly as could be . . . Despite all this, no light ever came through that would turn the wooden panel into a mirror; and even, thought the alchemist as he bent over his task, into far more than that. For the world's light is but a reflection of the veritable light—isn't this so? Even high noon is only a shadow. Each time he finished his work and stepped back, with anxious, questioning eyes, all he saw was grey, an indefinite grey. Just grey, even if at times that shadow seemed very white, like a sunny spell between two rains.

The stubborn seeker was growing old, and he'd tired of his quest; he even went so far as to interrupt it now and then, for several days. All the same, one morning he dripped from a vial yet another drop of colour on the useless mix. His numbed attention was suddenly called to the fore: before knowing why, he felt a sudden surge of hope.

Maybe it was because, near a dab of very dark, very saturated red, a brighter value had appeared by contrast—which led him to believe there was something like a gleam in the indeterminate mud of the other colour. Later, he couldn't remember what he'd thought or imagined in that minute; but after some hesitation, he'd applied a daub of saffron yellow next to the red splotch. Then he stood back from the panel, which by now he'd propped up against a wall. With his eyes half-closed, he looked at the two colours side by side. God knows why, he was reminded of a field drenched with water he'd seen one evening, at sunset: he'd been troubled by the two colours that collided there in the shadows. After wavering once more, he placed a third colour beside the other two, a blue—perhaps because of stones he'd observed in the stream that drained the pools at the bottom of the field.

Three spots now, that almost touch! And they give off a beam that isn't just the greyness of matter stirred in vain—but isn't quite the simple sun, either, as it edged the field on that first day.

We meet the alchemist again a few weeks later, feverishly exploring the iridescence wrought by opposing colours on the grey background, on the patches of light and dark. From now on, he's convinced that at certain moments this contrast heats up, intensifies, as if a glowing force pressed against it, possibly from a fire that strives to penetrate matter through this path. He came to think that it isn't from the mixture of colours, utterly material, but from their juxtaposition—which unites them at a higher level—that one day, abruptly perchance, a streak of lightning will be born.

And now at last—though years have passed—he's completed his task. The ray of light shines with mystery; it peacefully burns in the vessel of his great work: the wooden panel, resting against the wall, he's kept before him for such a long time. We look over his shoulder, sympathetically. Has he really done nothing more than study the bonds between values, between tones? It seems to us we're gazing at a fairly free rendition of a field of maize, or sunflowers, at dusk beside a stream; or else it's a marsh, where blue water has flooded the clumps of yellow blooms. Have we just witnessed a grand moment of history—of the mind? In which the alchemist of colour may have invented landscape painting?

He's taken the picture in his hands, and he's going to set it on a small pile of stones—since we're outside, I should've said. For a long time, he's been working in front of his door, near these stones blackened as if by sacrifice. And it's here, too, that this field begins; at present, its far end trails off into the crimson clouds of evening. He sets the picture down, and steps back once again—but happy now, satisfied. Then he turns around. Three angels are standing there, who look at him and smile. One wears a red robe; another's raiment is blue-grey; the third is swathed in saffron yellow, inconceivably vivid and intense. 'Who are you?' he asks them.

'We are the Earth,' they answer. 'The Earth that you create. We've come to sit with you under the arbour. Offer us some bread and wine. We need to speak for quite a while, my friend, before the fall of night.'

The Wandering Life

For several days, he strove to be content with the clouds on his canvas: he'd banked them above a path of stone. But what is beauty when we know we'll move on? Tomorrow, the boat will convey him to another island. He'll never return to this one; he'll never see this path again.

Suddenly, he trembled with anguish and dropped his brush; it spattered the bottom of his painting with a dash of dark ochre, almost red. Ah, what joy!

On the Jordan's bank after his lengthy voyage, what can Chateaubriand do but fill a flask with the river's water? He writes on a label: Water from the Jordan.

Splotch—epiphany of what has no meaning, has no form—you are the unforeseen gift I possessively carry off, leaving the vain picture incomplete. You will enlighten me, you will save me.

Aren't you a fragment of the real, of this instant and this place? A particle of gold, where I'd only aspired to the reflection that betrays, the memory that rips apart? I've torn a scrap from the dress that slips from childhood's fingers, eluding their grasp like a dream.

All Morning in the City

He left his hotel very early, with what he thought was an illustrated guide to the city. He crossed the river on a bridge built in the century when that city had achieved its independence, newly focused on the future and on architectural grace. On the other shore were the monuments of this resplendence, severe as to their facades; and yet a wild excess, so he was told, all chimeras and great bursts of colour, lay hidden on the other side—silent, empty—of their heavy doors.

Between two of these edifices, here's a street that leads behind them into scenes of ordinary life, up to the ramparts. It can only be a rather untidy clutter of houses, as a lot of time has gone by since the initial period of grandeur; hence the rundown, abandoned aspects. But there were fresh beginnings as well: new buildings jutting out at the crossroads, and even some innovative styles. And that's exactly what he beholds; yet there are so many

20

facets he hadn't foreseen! He'd imagined bare walls, and high windows with fitted grills; on the contrary, all he discovers is low, cramped shops—quite silent, it's true. They're the kind you have to come up close to, pressing your forehead against the glass, so you can make out what's on display, such as a vague little flame in a mirror's pool, untouched by the sun. As to the street itself, it's longer, much longer than he'd thought, with side streets cutting through it again and again. These offer him other neighbourhoods he sometimes explores, suddenly attracted by a half-concealed chapel, or a shaft of sun at the far end of a dark passageway. But he comes back fairly soon, because these new streets branch off in turn, revealing still more chapels, more lofty stairways under colonnades, more of those princely mansions with their heavy, studded doors—where violent knocks had been struck now and then, the thuds resounding for ages in the depths of vacant rooms.

Yes, he retraces his steps: he always returns to the street he'd wanted to follow, glad he succeeds in finding his way. Yet these spaces never stop seeming vaster to him than he'd realized; he even begins to think perhaps they're expanding, as he moves forward under the morning sky.

The sky itself appears to stand still: a scale balanced between two azure weights. Everything multiplies, fans out. He reaches the point where he perceives afar, on the city heights—admittedly rather dark—passers-by who're tinted by the bright hues of memory. That man, for example, or that woman. The man walks forward, offering his hand with a smile; but at the last moment, where is he? And the woman's figure, so vague from the start—though she makes gestures and calls out, in her phosphorescent dress beneath a hat of light . . . They were there, or almost. Hello, goodbye: he must press on in this street that increases, stretches out, fades away.

It remains quite narrow, all the same, with bookshops here along its steep, downhill slope. The traveller walks right into them, since he's noted they only contain the piled-up glimmers of stones, often dusty; or leftover timberwork, broken and blackened, with shreds of cloth that also show up amid the disarray; or sheets of paper where several words are legible, who can say, between the adjacent burns imprinted by fire long ago. Shift those joists, those stones. Extract from their depths this little steel wristwatch, tarnished now, with its ribbon of black silk and dainty hands: the very one the wanderer's mother used to lay on the mantelpiece beside the clock every evening. Two tick-tocks that answered each other, that merged; but only the ear of God could've heard the weaker of the two from where the child slept, and could've mulled over their nearness in the night.

Let's leave these memories behind, and go on into the depths of the shop, where we find the street once again that keeps descending; and at the bottom now, nearby, is the river's light.

Soon I'm on the quay, where I meet with luminosity on every side. I see the great river retreat into the distance: no longer as it was in the early morning, but instead an immense body of water, between banks very broad themselves—like avenues with numberless vehicles streaming by, noiseless and glittering. Across the river, far-away under the light-blue sky, are the superb monuments of the opposite shore—steeples and domes. And before me, this bridge with the same proportions as the quays and the river, with the same vehicles, the same passers-by like floating shades of evanescent hues. No, they don't exist, nor does the bridge. Maybe only the water is real; it surges from every direction, amplified even more. I survey the magnificent panorama: the city seems limitless, infinite.

I've forgotten the name of my hotel, and what street it's on as well; I only know that it's somewhere over there, so I'll have to cross the river. But on the horizon, to my right, I catch sight of the little bridge I went over when this morning began, and now I head that way.

The Northern Fire

I admire the definition of poetry in *Beasts*, *Men and Gods*, the inexhaustible book by Ossendowski. It's in the first pages, when he's decided to flee across Siberia all alone, along the Yenisei. And he's afraid; he lingers in the mountains, his mind still fixed on his past—a past that's coming to an end, beneath stars that already loom closer . . . Suddenly, someone unknown to him appears, without a sound, on the threshold of the cabin where he's sheltering. This stranger offers to guide him for a while, in the immensity under the snow.

And so they set out. 'We spent that night in the woods, beneath the wide, spreading branches of the firs. It was my first night in the forest, in the great outdoors. How many nights like this I was destined to spend in the eighteen months of my wandering life! [. . .] We came to a halt in a deep ravine, bordered by thick trees; there we found some fallen firs, and cut them into logs [. . .] Ivan dragged two tree trunks over, squared them off along one side with his axe, and set them atop each other by joining the two squared sides. Then he stuck big wedges between their ends, dividing them by three or four inches. We put burning coals into this opening, and watched the fire run swiftly along the entire length of the squared sides, set face to face.'

'Now there'll be fire till tomorrow morning,' he told me. This is the *naïda*, the northern fire of solitary travellers.

Strabo the Geographer

He reads the description left by Strabo, the geographer, of the world that he knew.

The world is no more than a vast expanse of grasses, says Strabo. Plain after plain, stretching into the infinite. A few trees, in the distance. Some water under our footsteps, shallow among the stones.

And now and then a fire, flush with the horizon. First, we'll see its smoke, in the ebbing sun. Then we'll arrive at a camp. Silently, children play. Men and women speak of Catullus or Boetius, in quiet voices. Suddenly a woman stands up, head bowed, and draws the curtain of a tent.

Glaucus the God

I write, but once again my pen goes astray, and once again—what would it end up saying, if I didn't hold it back?—starts the sentence: 'A tearful voice, wandering through the rocks . . .'

I listen. The voice seems to shout that one of the rocks is Glaucus, so disfigured by time, sea and storms that 'he's no longer a god any more, only a savage beast.'

I cross out these few words, I refuse. Yes, that's a beach. Here and there, smooth boulders tower high; behind their hulking blackness, others loom. And the sand between them flows like bright water, soundless from now on, along the surface of the world.

As Far as I Know You

—I know your name, she told him.

—How so? I have no name.

—I know where you come from, she told him.

—How so? Where could I have been, to come from there?

And he added, from the threshold, leaning against the stones the sun had warmed—though with his head and shoulders backlit, edged by the evening's ochre red—that he had no face, no eyes, no rhyme or reason in his words; that he didn't exist.

She was smiling even so, mysteriously self-assured, enfolded by the airy dress of happiness for all eternity— slightly stirred by something like a breeze.

The Clock

With a finger, he tried to pry the clock's hands from its dial, but they were so rusty they'd stuck to the metal plate. Or no, instead they'd been painted on slight ridges that suggested their relief. The clock was only an image: this ten past noon bespoke the timelessness of an image, not the vestige of a bygone duration.

Besides, in the garden around it, the fruits ripened well outside that hour. The cricket also had its way of erasing any idea, any memory of time; yet its chirpy rasping would stop sometimes, then begin again. In our first days, admittedly, those hesitations instilled us with brief surges of hope.

Sugarfoot

I'd been at my friends' house for several hours—a beautiful and happy house, with a dog richly reflecting an abundance of goodness, and of serious depth. To be sure, the big, faithful dog was a bit distracted that day, and quite restless; she'd go out often, then come back, only to leave once again. She'd just given birth to a litter of small lives: you could see them hopping clumsily beneath the porch, on a bed of straw. Her name was Sugarfoot.

We were chatting, talking excitedly, walking along the paths and around the rooms. Still more friends had arrived, some from far away, very far away.

Suddenly I heard a sentence inside myself: 'There was a dog in that place named Sugarfoot.' Right after that, everything seemed different from the minute before: not discoloured—instead, more transparent, to the point of appearing unreal. In fact, the beginnings of a story spread like fire in the density of the moment, which till then had only been lived naively. Of the sun and shadows, the faces and voices, nothing remained but ashes, the ashes of memory.

I was afraid of this power I possessed.

But looking around me—listening, though not hearing: 'Ah! I said to myself, I'm not the only one who's guilty! We're all complicit in this lie: forgetfulness. As we laugh, as we talk, we're swimming side by side in the water that dissolves us, and which makes the future tale get the better of us—since it is already ourselves, more completely than we are, perhaps. We need to cease moving forward like this, eyes shut.'

And I imagined myself crying out—though of course, with my empty hands, I did nothing of the kind: 'Let's stop! Let's freeze our gestures for a moment! From this crossroads, let's head off again in another way! Since her name is Sugarfoot. Do you understand? Do you truly understand her name is Sugarfoot?

'Forever, she's the only one here today whose name is Sugarfoot.'

Impressions at Sunset

This evening, the painter they call a storm
Has done good work: exquisite figures
Gather to the left beneath a portico
Of sky, where phosphorescent stairs
Drop down to the sea. And in this throng
There is a stir, as though a god had just appeared,
A golden face those darker ones surround.

Their chorus of surprise, almost a chant,
Their laughter and the music of the fifes—
They reach us not as sound, but shapes of sound.
Their arms, thrown open, multiply and break,
Their widened gestures dilate and dissolve,
And colour moults from shade to shade
Beyond all colour, without end,
Spinning islands in the air
And shattered organ pipes of cloud. Is this

The resurrection of the dead? Then it must be
The final cresting of the waves, before they tumble down.
The sky is almost empty now.
A ruddy mass slouches north
Towards a curtain of black birds, twittering: night.

Here and there
A puddle struck by an ember
Of beauty burnt to ash.

Huge Red Rocks

He wondered how he could say these slabs of rock, huge and red; this grey, silvery water that glided between them in silence; this sombre lichen, at different heights on the jumbled stones. He wondered what words could enter the rugged crevices, as his gaze was doing in this very moment . . . what words could partake of the raddled bushes under low-hanging branches, before this cliff edge that dropped away beneath his steps—amid more brambles, more outcrops of sandstone with rust-coloured spots . . . Why is there no term to denote, in just a few syllables, these swirls of dead leaves and dust, stirred by the breeze? Or another to denote by itself, in a way as specific as it is precise, the instant when a gnat breaks away from the swarm, above the rotten plums on the grass, and then comes back? This is a loop lived out with no awareness, a sign bereft of meaning—a fact bereft of being, too: and yet an absolute, all the same, in itself as vast as the whole abyss of the sky. And these clouds, as they're arrayed at the present moment—their colours and their shapes? And these sand-flows in the grass near the stream? And this slight cocking of the blackbird's head, when he's alighted for no reason, and for no reason will fly away? How can it be that language has consented to approach so few aspects of the world—not to toil over knowledge, but to find repose in the dreaminess of the real, resting its head on the shoulder of things with eyes closed? What a loss it is, to name . . . What a lure, to speak . . . And what a task befalls us when we question ourselves before the earth we love, the earth we would like to say . . . What an endless task, simply to be at one with the earth . . . a task we conceive from childhood on . . . We live by dreaming it possible, and die from knowing it can't be achieved!

He walked on, skirting a big red boulder that loomed as if alone on a pool of sand. He took a few steps on the other side of the rock, now on even ground, almost bare; at the edge, some water softly lapped, its depths almost blue . . . And he understood, then and there, that he'd badly posited the problem of being and words. To raise words to the power of being, it wasn't the sudden cocking of the blackbird's head we needed to capture by a newfound term—any more than the rustle of foliage in the nearby oaks, or the sandstone's veins when they show up at certain points beneath the brambles and dry leaves. These successive foci of his attention were but flimsy effigies, which the words he possessed had detached from a background. Its only reality was undifferentiated; its only visibility was immersed—or almost—in the sweeping currents of the invisible. He'd be far better off if he could draw on other words, words whose naming would delete the maximum number of futile distinctions: these merely encumbered his gaze, all in all. Words which by that token would commence, in our encounter with the world, what the landscape-painter's brush achieves: as when it seizes, in a single crimson stroke, not only all the meadow's poppies but myriad other plants as well, and even an entire bend in this path that wends its way.

Now he dreams of a word that would say all at once, would indistinctly say both the gnat and the whirling leaf, and also the water from the spring, and a little blackbird tilting its head that's just alighted close to him on a branch. And of another word, which this time would denote that lichen over there, growing halfway up between the base and the summit of the world, and the play of foam on a swollen wave which already falls back, and all the stars of summer nights . . . Yes, all that, thereby reduced to the one and only idea we sense so well—don't you think?—beneath the pleats and creases of the evident. Words that would dissolve the illusion of difference as a painter's colours do, allowing those harmonies a picture transmutes into light. Words that would simplify, magnify, intensify, offering us anew what as children our lips have drunk: this breast that is what is, on the inner side of time and space, as soon as the eager hand has freed it from the scarf of our words, too heavy up till now.

He dreams like this, as he keeps walking forward. And still later, if we know how to catch up with him, he will tell us—smiling, but with his eyes fixed on the ground, where certain stones shine with tiny mosses, turning purple as night falls—that since words must do the work that colours in landscape painting do so well, it's only logical for them to reveal themselves as equally few. Twenty or thirty, let's say, or even only three fundamental hues. From their fusion, duly proportioned in moments of experience we might call poems—just as emerald green arises from a certain yellow and a blue—those categories of perception would come to the fore, those aspects of the palpable world we must decide upon, no doubt, because they're born where we are: so that there, we can live our allotted time; and so that there, we can die.

Three words, only three words to say what is: what repose, what blissful sleep against this great breathing body the most serious and secret of our painters have let us glimpse, those priests of eternal Isis! Where we had dreaded, in a moment of vertigo, the infinite multiplication of terms, now we find these three angels standing at our threshold, more visible at evening, to be sure, when their multicoloured wings stand out against the early stars. —The three theological virtues, in this religion of the West that knows so little of stones, or of the mosses that glow on them at night—perhaps from their origin they only transposed the desire we've always nurtured for those three simple words, and our inkling of the equally simple mode of being that would assure our fulfilment, our happiness, as soon as the true language might be discovered, or relearnt. As soon as we could never stray but three steps—among the red rocks, on the grass mingled with sand—from the intimacy of silence.

Landscape with the Flight into Egypt

I was in a taxi on the way to Logan Airport. It was dawn, and we were rolling through the Boston suburbs, still almost deserted. All the same, at a street corner, I briefly glimpsed a young woman with a child in her arms, and beside her a stooped, elderly man; they stood back from the pavement to let the car pass. They seemed weary. Their clothes looked indefinably foreign to that country—to the world, perhaps. When I turned around, I saw that a donkey had joined them in the middle of the road. Their few possessions were tied in a bundle to its back, under a red cape of sorts.

More suburbs, factories, the brick walls of old houses with black windows. I'm sorely tempted not to continue, to leave the car behind and walk at random through these streets where there would be an obelisk . . . and on the horizon what seem to be pyramids . . . and that's where the man and woman would turn up, now wearing huge straw hats. The Nile flows peacefully, irresistibly, behind these porticoes; above them the sky is blue because time has ceased to exist.

Ten days ago, in New York, de Kooning's paintings closed all exits, put an end to the world. I had a dream during the night that has just passed. Somewhere, I'm giving a public reading. Is it Phoenix, where my plane is going? But I'll be getting out in Chicago . . . And it happens that out of the blue, I read in my own book a word whose meaning is unknown to me, then sentences I'm certain I never wrote—which, moreover, make no sense. After that, the book itself vanishes from my sight, and everything lapses into a blur.

Yesterday evening, *The Changing Rains* attained an absolute beauty. Just a small documentary film—with no pretentions, in fact—about a group of aborigines in their South Indian enclave. But the expanses of the enormous plain, with infinite shots of copses veiled by mist . . . and these children, these young people dancing as they hold each other's shoulders, almost motionless, their gazes lost . . . Space shifts beneath the rain, shifts within the rooms filmed as well, owing to the awkward camera work. That goddess in gilded wood, carried just now in a procession under the trees . . . it's as if we're seeing the world through her eyes.

Noon in Chicago, with a lot of fog; a red van shuttles between the planes on the tarmac—the sole spot of colour amid the greyness. In Cedar Rapids, I'm expecting to see *The Wedding of Bacchus and Ariadne*, the superb canvas by Poussin—but the winds will soon reroute our flight. We're obliged to land at Quad Cities Airport. What cities it serves I'll never know, since I've been advised to take a long-range bus towards Des Moines right away—one that passes, or so I'm told, through that other Iowa town where I'm awaited.

Night has fallen. The motorcoach has been cruising along for quite a while, in this plain marked by only a few sparse lights—besides those, rare in themselves, of the cars on the highway. And then I learn we won't drive through my destination after all, since I'm the only traveller going there; but I'll be let off at a restaurant on the outskirts, as near as possible. A few more miles. I suspect I'm going to forget *The Changing Rains*; nothing of it will remain but this light stippled by water that covers the windows of the bus, in which every lamp has been turned off. Sometimes another vehicle coasts beside us for a spell, then passes us, or else we pass it. Before me, a windscreen wiper sweeps unhurriedly the foreground of the sky, where there's a reddish gleam—as if that were India over there, or Egypt in the middle of nowhere.

All the Gold in the World

He awakens from the dream where he'd been the alchemist
of colour . . . And so, the vessel's gold will go missing
forever, as proved by this daylight, faint and grey against
the windowpanes. In their water, the branches and leaves
of green, of red, of blue hardly budge, mere shadows of
that more intensive colour that he'd sensed, that he'd even
thought he'd glimpsed. How cramped everything is here,
how badly everything breathes . . . There's so much black
sand in this handful of silt the blind god has shaped! Only
the shouts of children at their game, over there, attest that
gold shines now and then in the sand.

Gold—a flank of the world where we might enter into
death, if need be . . . like passing through high, luminous
bushes, then trees with low branches, laden with fruit.
Touch the fruits, gather them in baskets; walk on amid the
scent of flowers and grass; picnic later, on inlets of bright
sand, and taste the happiness of a day such as this: in the
summer night, it can only end with a sudden sleep, your

head resting on a folded arm. Yes, this gold does exist after all in the mirror's depths, since we see specks of it slip from a sleeping child's fingers as they unclench—as he murmurs indistinct words, on this side of his dream.

THE GRAPES OF ZEUXIS

The Grapes of Zeuxis

A wet canvas ragbag in the gutter: it's the picture of grapes by Zeuxis, which enraged birds craved so much, picked apart so fiercely with their greedy beaks, that the clusters vanished, then the colours, then every trace of the image at this hour—the twilight of the world—when they dragged it across the flagstones.

The Dogs

A land of mountains that are dogs, valleys that are barks, boulders erect in those barks, like dogs who strain at the end of their chains.

And in their jumps, their pants, their fury, here is the open door, and the spacious room. The fire is bright, the table is set; the wine gleams in the carafes.

The Top of the World

The sky's weight on the glass became unbearable; it was said you could hear appearance crack. Someone shouted that in . . . X, they'd seen 'the unknown' issue forth—men and women, perfectly beautiful and nude—while the top of the world, of a blacker and blacker blue, toppled and fell like a stone.

Night

Night, that is the green, the blues, and this dash of very dark red, nipping the lowest part of the page with its lumps. Hastily, I write the word puddle, the word star. I write birth. I write shepherds and three kings. I write that I break a light bulb, and this is black.

The Task of Non-existence

They told him of a civilization graced with all the skills of the marble cutter, the smelter; it was heir to a classical art, given to placing korai and nude ephebes at the crossroads of its cities, in the penumbra of its temples. But this new era no longer wanted statues—only empty pedestals; sometimes fires were lit on them, bent by winds from the sea. The philosophers said these bare plinths were the sole works of value: they had taken on, among the gullible crowds, the task of non-existence.

The Blind Man

He gazed fixedly at the sun, as it set among red clouds. But how could we have addressed him, since he was no more than this large statue of honey-coloured marble some of us carried on our shoulders, with greater and greater fatigue? Since his ecstatic gesture towards the sun swayed accordingly, lunging up and down like the prow of a boat? Since his expression—that of a blind singer— was already ebbing from the stone, like the fire from those distant red clouds?

The Incision

It's simple: you dip a finger into the blue gouache, you slide it along the words just traced in black ink, and from the mixture of ink and colour a tide wells up. Algae stir in the cloudy water, no longer the sign, no longer the image— our two passions, our two lures. We've opened our eyes; we move forward in the light of dawn.

But I wake up. Before me, on the wall of layered colours that flake off, there's a shape deeply engraved with a nail, down to the plaster. Does it evoke a lamb, carried by a god on his shoulders? Or is the figure obscene? In fact, the incision goes so far into the plaster's night that its empty rim is all that counts: a gash through any quest for images, an erasure of any sign.

The Book

Light fidgets in the cellar: I'm told they've found something, the children down there. They're trying to bring it up to us on the narrow ladder, through the trapdoor. What is it? We don't quite know yet—something like 'a book', an 'endless' book, 'the book'. As I lean over the highest rungs, still badly lit, I catch sight of their faces, bobbing back and forth to see me better. Laughing, singing . . . you'd think they were angels. I reach out my arms, and soon my hands overflow with masses of grey pages, stitched with coarse red thread; and sand that sifts through my fingers; and bits of wood, some of them rotten; and stones.

They Spoke to Me

.

They told me: no, don't pick that up; don't touch that, it'll burn. No, don't try to touch that, don't hold on; it's too heavy, it'll hurt.

They told me: read, write. And I tried, I picked up a word; but it struggled, clucking like a frightened, wounded hen—in a cage of black straw, stained by old traces of blood.

THE GRAPES OF ZEUXIS AGAIN

Incompletable

When he was twenty years old, he lifted up his eyes and looked at the sky. He looked at the earth again—with attention. So it was true! God had only sketched the world: he'd left nothing there but ruins.

A ruin, this oak, so beautiful all the same. A ruin, this water, lapping so softly against the bank. A ruin, the sun itself. All these signs of beauty are ruins—as the clouds prove so well, more beautiful still.

Perhaps light alone has a fully fledged life, he said to himself. That's why it seems simple, uncreated. —Since then, in the oeuvre of painters, he only loves their sketches. For him, the stroke closing back on itself betrays the mission of that god, who placed the anguish of the quest above the joy of the finished work.

The Painter's Despair

He was painting: the slope of a mountain, the serried ochre stones. But this homespun cloth parted to uncover a breast, where a child was pressing its lips. And the heights, almost the sky, descended into the night (for night had come), where coffers were being carried, that leaked glimmers of light.

How many pictures did he leave like that, unfinished, invaded! The years passed; his hand shook. The landscape-painter's work was no more than those slabs of shiny coal piled up over there, where the children of heaven and earth kept wandering.

The Museum

A hue and cry, far away. A crowd that runs under pouring rain, between canvases rattled by gales from the sea.

A man rushes by, shouting. What does he say? That he knows . . . that he's seen! I make out his words. Ah, I almost understand.

I've found refuge in a museum. Henceforth, the great windy rain reigns alone outside, shaking the windows.

In each painting, it seems to me, God refuses to finish the world.

Nocturnal Justice

I dream that all I remember of world painting is *The Mocking of Ceres* by Adam Elsheimer, and *Diana and her Companions* by Vermeer.

It's 'nocturnal justice'. Now I'm very close to her. She turns her small, childlike face towards me; she laughs beneath her dishevelled hair.

Homage

I had to pay homage. In a second, I had to decide who among us had practised supreme rigor, and supreme imprudence all at once.

And in the night, I shouted out the name 'Nicolas Poussin'. I pressed forward down the hallway—where there was smoke, verging on flames—up to a threshold that gleamed with light.

I entered: there he lay, amid patches of rubble and mud. I shouted again: 'No, don't die!' I took his hand in the abyss of long-lost time, of vain beliefs, of baffling images, of the dead god. I guided it towards the brush that had rolled to the ground—beside the canvas whose whole left half is blank, in the absolute.

The Great Image

It was the temple. The door: low and narrow; the walls of the hallway: grey and clammy. Hidden at the back, beside the cellar stairs, the gate of the lift was so heavy it slid shut with a clang. The upper storeys seemed empty—closed, even walled off—except for this door on the third floor.

The altar is there, in the little dining room: it's a spigot with water running.

And the image is there on the altar: the great, divine image. You can touch it; you can hold it in your hands; you can knead it under the water in the sink. It's a clump of soft earth. You can work it easily into countless shapes, though at times a few pieces come loose. You gather them up again; you press them back into the lump, infinitely grey and sad; you mould it again into a ball.

The Crucifix

They show him a large crucifix in the chapel to the left. They recount how an elderly man brought it to them one evening, bent beneath its weight.

He said he would pick it up again the next day, but he never returned. And since then, everything out there—the street, the passers-by at times—is plunged into night. Florence: that's where God came from; it's the other world.

The head leans on one shoulder. Blood from the crown of thorns leaves a red stain on the grey wood. A cleft starts at the shoulder, and seeks out the heart; it sunders the marks of suffering, seems to make them fade.

The Grapes of Zeuxis Again

Zeuxis painted—by fending off the famished birds with his left arm. But they even darted under his jostled brush, to tear out scraps of canvas.

He contrived to hold a torch—again in his left hand—that spewed black smoke of the thickest kind. His eyes blurred; he could no longer see. He should've been painting badly; by now his grapes shouldn't evoke anything on earth. So why did the birds throng more fiercely, more voraciously than ever? They swooped at his hands and at the image. They went so far as to bite his fingers, making them bleed on the blue, the amber green, the ochre red.

He contrived to paint in the dark. He wondered what these forms must look like, as he let them collide, mix together, disappear, in the basket's ill-defined ring. But the birds knew. They perched on his fingers. Their beaks poked holes in the unknown picture his brush encountered, moving more slowly than they.

He contrived to leave off painting. He'd wanted to add a few fruits to the world: from two steps away, he merely gazed at their absence. Some birds flew about in the distance. Others alighted on the branches before his window; still others, on his jars of various hues.

She Who Invented Painting

As for the daughter of the Corinth potter, she's long ago renounced her aim of drawing her lover's outline on the wall, by tracing her finger around his shadow. She reclines on her bed, as the candle projects a fanciful crest of twisted sheets against the plaster. She turns around, with eyes fulfilled, towards the shape she's broken with her embrace. 'No, I won't prefer the image to you,' she says. 'I won't deliver you up as an image, to the swirls of smoke that thicken around us. You won't be that cluster of fruits, squabbled over in vain by the birds called forgetfulness.'

LAST GRAPES OF ZEUXIS

I

Zeuxis, despite the birds, didn't succeed in ridding himself of his desire—rightful, to be sure. In peace, he wanted to paint some clusters of blue grapes in a basket.

He'd been bloodied by eternally rapacious beaks, his canvases shredded by their dreadful impatience. Eyes burnt by the smoke with which he thwarted them in vain, he continued his work all the same. You'd think he perceived, in the ever-denser clouds of soot—where colour was blotted out, where form was broken up—something more than colour or form.

II

He caught his breath, at times. He sat a few steps from his easel among the thrushes, among the eagles and other raptors. They calmed down as soon as he stopped painting, and almost seemed to fall asleep. Weighed down by their feathers, they chittered vaguely now and then, in the odour of their droppings.

He pondered. How could he rise in silence, and approach the canvas—without space tilting again, all at once, into beating wings and countless hoarse cries?

III

And what a surprise it was as well, that late afternoon when he jumped up, seized a brush, and dipped it in red. Ordinarily, there would've been a scramble already, and shrieks of rage! But his hand trembled as he observed that this time, the birds were ignoring him.

Yet they were grapes, all the same, he was starting to paint: two clusters, two clusters almost full. Yesterday the unerring beaks would've still ripped away the very last fibre that bore a smidgeon of colour.

IV

Not even those weighty clusters, as it turned out . . . just one of the disguises he'd essayed, now and then, in order to deceive the hunger of the world. In the same way, he'd sketched—naively, of course—grapes striped with blue or pink, others that were cubes, others shaped like Terminus the god, plunged in his big beard. In vain, in vain! None of his projects had time to take shape. They devoured each idea directly from his mind: they snatched it from his hand as he attempted to near the canvas. As if, in the inexhaustible nature of the striated grapes—or of the stony, six-sided fruits, tossed on the table in defiance of chance—there might be clusters like marble statues for the birds' delight.

V

Now, he paints in peace. He can render his clusters more lifelike, more appetizing; he can cover them with the tender mist that makes their gold—iridescent with grey and blue—stand out so attractively against the basket's straw.

Emboldened, he even reaches the point where he places real grapes beside him, as in former days. A sparrow, a thrush—is that a thrush, then?—may occasionally alight on the rim of the actual basket; but he shoos them away with his hand, and those birds don't return.

VI

Long, long hours with nothing but his work, in silence. Before his house, the birds have resumed their wide circles, high in the sky. When they veer close to Zeuxis, who comes to paint on the terrace, they do so with indifference—the same as if they were brushing past a clump of thyme, or a rock.

It's true that once a resplendent troupe of parrots and hoopoes gathered on the terraces nearby, and loudly squawked with what he thought was rage. But an hour later, by common accord, the parrots and hoopoes and thrushes had left.

VII

Ah, what's happened? he wonders. Has he lost any sense of what fruits are like; or does he no longer know how to desire—how to live? That's hardly probable. Visitors drop by, to take a look. 'What beautiful grapes!' they say. And even: 'You've never painted grapes as lovely and lifelike as these.'

Or again, he wonders once more, was he sleeping? Was he dreaming? At the very moment when the birds tore his fingers, ate his colours, perhaps he'd been seated in a corner of his darkened studio, nodding off.

But now, why isn't he sleeping any more? In what world might he have awakened? Why does he miss his days of struggle and anguish, as he surely feels that he does? Why has he reached the point where he wishes to stop painting? And even, that painting should cease to exist?

VIII

Zeuxis wanders through the countryside. He picks up stones, tosses them back on the ground. He returns to his studio, takes up his brushes. His whole body trembles when a bird, swift as an arrow, comes to snatch one of the grapes from the basket. Then he waits, goes to the window and watches the large, migratory flocks choose a roof. Far away, over there in the evening light, they reduce the dimming sun's cluster to blue dust.

Strange, the bird that alighted yesterday, on the sill of this same window. It was multicoloured; it was grey. It had raptor's eyes; but for a head, it had tranquil waters that mirrored the clouds. Was it bringing a message? Or is the nothing of this world simply a ball of feathers, that bristle when the beak hunts for a flea?

IX

It's something akin to a puddle, the last picture Zeuxis painted—after long reflection, when he was declining already towards death. A puddle, a brief thought of calm, shining water . . . and if you leant over it, you glimpsed the shadows of grapes. At their edge, vaguely gilded, was the whimsical outline stitched in children's eyes by a cluster among the vines, when the twilit sky is luminous still.

Before those bright shadows are other shadows—black. But if you dip your hand in the mirror and stir this water, the shadows of birds and fruits will merge.

FROM WIND AND SMOKE

I

The Idea, some have thought, is the measure of all things.
If that were true, then Guido Reni's famous painting—
'La sua bella Elena rapita', Bellori called it—
Might compare to the other Helen: the Helen
Zeuxis depicted; the Helen he may have loved.
But what are such images, beside the real
Woman desired by Paris? Isn't the actual vine
This trembling of hands under fever's lips?
Why else would a child demand these grapes
So greedily? Why else would he make haste
To gulp the cluster down, to drink the light
Before the flood of time unfurls?

No, not at all, a commentator wrote,
Anxious to explain away
Ten years of war in the *Iliad*.
The truth is, Helen was never kidnapped;

She wasn't dragged, screaming, from boat to ship,
And chained to roughed-up beds.
An image was all the ravisher carried off,
A statue wrought by some magician's art
From the calm breezes of a summer eve:
So she would radiate their warmth,
And breathe with them like flesh—
So her eyes would reflect desire.
Helen's effigy
Wanders dreaming through the low arches
Of the fleeing ship. She seems to hear
The purling of another sea
In her blue veins; she seems content.
Other scholiasts have even thought
She was a sculpture made of stone.
In the cabin, jostled by squalls
Day after day, Helen's figure
Lies half-risen from her sheets,
Or from her dreams—and smiling,
Almost. She folds an arm
Gracefully against her breast.
The rising sun, the setting sun
Meander on her nakedness,

Then fade away. Later, on the high
Terrace of Troy, she keeps that smile.
But who—besides Paris, perhaps—
Has ever seen her? All the bearers knew
Was a huge reddish stone, cracked and rugged.
Cursing, drenched in sweat, they had to haul it
To the ramparts, in front of night.

A crumbling rock, the sand of origin:
Is this Helen, then? These clouds, these ruddy gleams:
Are they in the soul, or the sky?

Even Stesichorus wouldn't admit
The truth; but maybe it was this:
Helen's semblance was just a fire,
Built against the wind on a beach—
A skein of grey branches and smoke
From sputtering flames. At the dew point
Of dawn, Paris heaped the sodden bonfire
On a boat, ravaged by waves and ringed
By screeching seabirds.
He kindled it again on his native shores,
Where breakers slashed and gouged
The shoals anew. Above, against the sky,

He'd raised the bed of stone.
The day Troy fell, a fire would remain
To shout of beauty—the only protest
Of the spirit against death.

Clouds . . .
One catches at another, that can't resist.
And between these bodies in love,
From its glittering cup,
A thunderbolt spills out.

The sky
Lingers for a while
On the bed of earth. The water, the mountain:
They seem like a woman, a man.
Between them,
The cup is already empty, and still full.

II

But this woman Paris embraced—this fire
And the branches red within the fire,
The hollow sockets bitter with smoke—
Who can say? Was she the dream
Behind the work that slakes the artist's thirst—
Or merely a dream of that dream?
Helen's smile: only a fold in the cloth of night,
Slipping to reveal how light still sleeps
Beneath the sky,
For a lightning flash.

Helen melts away
Every time a poem,
A statue, even a painted image
Tries to become a figure, detached
From the fits and starts of the gleaming cloud.
She was merely an intuition Homer sought,

Plumbing the notes below his deepest strings
On the awkward lyre of earthly words.

But at the dawn of meaning—
When the stone is still obscure, when colour
Is still mud in the headlong brush—
Paris does carry Helen off;
And though she struggles and cries out,
She accepts. The hull moves calmly
Through the waves, like daybreak
Across the sea.

Drink, says Paris,
When he wakes, stretching out his arm,
As the cabin's narrow darkness
Rocks in a gentle swell.
Drink—
Then raise the cup to my lips
So I can drink as well.

I will, she answers; I will drink.
(Does she exist, or only as a dream?)
I have no name, no more than a cloud.
A cloud, I will dissolve in purest light.

And once I have given you joy, the light
Consumed, I will never thirst again.

From the wide beach, the day Troy burned,
A naked child
Was the last to see her: Helen,
A tree of flames on the upper wall.
He dawdled, he sang.
He cupped a little water in his hands,
Where the fire could come to drink.
But water seeps from the imperfect cup:
The dream is ruined by time; by time redeemed.

III

These pages are translations. From a tongue
That haunts the memory I have become.
Its phrases falter, like what we recollect
From early childhood, long ago.
I built the text again, word for word:
But mine is only shadow. As though we know
All origin is a Troy that burns,
All beauty but regret, and all our work
Runs like water through our hands.

A STONE

I still hunger for that place
That was our mirror, hunger
For the fruit curved in its waters,
Hunger for its saving light.

And in memory of how it shone,
I will now engrave a circle
On the rock, an empty fire.
The sky moves swiftly overhead,

As the stone closes to our vow.
What were we seeking? Nothing,
Perhaps. A passion is only a dream;
Its hands will never ask.

And whoever has loved an image:
Though his eyes may still desire,
His voice is broken;
His words are full of ash.

TWO MUSICIANS, THREE PERHAPS

Two Musicians, Three Perhaps

Almost motionless, this crowd on the esplanade at nightfall . . . so vast I see nothing that might be its end over there, on the other shore—if not perhaps these plumes of red smoke that carry colour into the sky, grey elsewhere, or at times almost black.

Here's a musician, trying to force his way through all these silent beings. He's playing a small violin; but with his shoulder or one of his knees he can push aside the ones who block his path—often without paying him any mind. How hard it is to go about all alone! Sometimes you have to stop short because two beings are talking to each other and never let up—jowl to jowl, with horror in their eyes and arms never ceasing to unravel, countless as they are, in the dark. At other moments, sight unseen, you have to step over bodies lying among people's legs—indifferent, all the same, or asleep. Behind the musician, his path closes up again. And before him? Before him, there's only night . . . not even the sound of a river.

The musician makes his way, in the crowd that grows denser and denser. He makes his way, but now he understands all of a sudden that far-off as yet, from this same side he's coming from—far-off and invisible, almost inaudible—another musician is also trying to forge ahead, perhaps to join up with him.

But that musician isn't just playing a small violin. His instrument is a light openwork frame, not unlike the basket of a hot-air balloon, with streamers that float in the wind from the ends of numberless rods. They truly bristle around a kind of sombre soul, which the musician over there holds between his hands—unless what appear to be his hands are the sun and moon, gravitating closer now in this sky of a changing world. A leather handle is attached to the lower end of the instrument—though it's hard to tell, the throng surrounds it so tightly! We think the handle serves to pull a cord from the depths of the soul; up there, in the wooden gondola, among the silk and paper ribbons, it provokes layers of bright sound: click-clacks trailing like laughter, breezes rustling through leaves, evanescent waves of yellow and red. The sound increases at times, and then there are children: they scamper under the thicket of grown-ups. They jostle each other; they even fall down in moments of panic. But then they stand up again, and try to make fires. They lift their round heads towards the musician when he passes by.

Is there a third musician, at a greater distance still—below the horizon? One who won't reach us till the night has fallen for good? When from that time forward the crowd grows colourless, feverless—when it lapses into its final whisperings? One who holds his instrument in both hands—no, who touches it with the tip of his finger, as if he were tracing signs in the steam on a windowpane . . . like the glass where as children, verging on sleep, we used to listen to the rain plash and plink. The summer rain was uneven: at times, a sudden downpour; at times, steady almost. Then it's two or three heavier drops, then a shower once more; and always it's different and always, even so, it's the same sound scattered, reunited, forgotten, detected all over again at the bottom of an instant, when the whole world is blotted out.

Three Memories of the Journey

I

I was looking at a picture—a landscape. I'd been told that finally—and 'undoubtedly', or 'obviously'—it evinced an aspect of another world. And I sought it out: I questioned these wide horizons, these masses of clouds, these trees with glittering leaves—yet all in vain. Must I resign myself to thinking, like Leonardo the painter, that the other world is nothing but the vulture, almost perfectly invisible, which gently holds in its talons our lights and colours: forever, the only that exist.

Time passed; they were preparing to store the picture in a cupboard.

And it was only at the last second, when they were already carrying it away, that I grasped how the enigma, or excess of evidence, had gathered at any rate within a certain green spot. Down in a trough, it was the shadow cast by a tree along a path. A low wall stood there as well, warmed by the full luminous red of what was now the evening sun.

II

Then I was trying to demist a window with the back of my hand.

But through it I made out something red, shrouded by multicoloured wings, armed with an immense beak and claws. It was screeching, though I couldn't hear its shrieks because the glass was too thick. I searched blindly for a handle to open the window, but all I found was the shape of a foot, a knee, a body. I surmised it was a Victory of pallid marble, veined by those momentous storms that sometimes illumine the night of the world.

Then I was taken by the hand and led into another room.

III

And now there's a rain like the crack of doom, in Seville.

I enter the museum. At the end of a room, its windows lashed by water, I catch sight of a statue: a young woman, in painted wood or stone. Almost at the level of her face she holds up a hand mirror, set in silver; on the mirror's back is yet another face, which smiles at me. A ray of sun, from who knows where, has fallen on the face that's supposedly real; and so the image within the image—although dark—is completely rimmed by light.

Later on, it's night. I'm at San Salvador. From a distance, I look at the chapel to the right of the choir, and raise my eyes. At the top of the wall, I see a shadow—immense, distended, since the bulb that's causing it burns too close to one of the retable's supports. The shadow is cast by a gilded wooden head, which a forgotten sculptor encircled with beams of light long ago.

Two Sentences, and Others

'He scoured the park's pathways in the radiant light of sunset, but without encountering a living soul; at last he ended up before the great room, and the sun's last rays, reflected in the mirror, dazzled him so fiercely that he couldn't recognize the two beings there . . .' Having reached this point in my reading, and feeling dazzled myself, I desist. The impression made on me is too intense: those two obscure patches moving behind the window-panes, under the light. They're like two beings who haunt our memory, shades on the banks of the Styx: not because of death at all, but because the unconscious (or at least, so we're told) harbours nothing more than symbols that interweave—symbols, not presences—in the workings of desire. 'Souls that live', on the contrary, are souls that live again, these 'two beings there'. And an encounter is poss-ible anew, in my future where what's been left off can be resumed, where perhaps the bonds of earlier times—

incomplete, consigned to silence—will deepen. The glass door is half-open, isn't it? Like water in spate, flowing more quickly, life will break loose from the side-drifts and whirlpools that hampered and thwarted its course.

I've stopped reading. And today, twelve years later, having found the yellow envelope where I'd hastily jotted this sentence on the back, I say to myself that perhaps great novels—like *Wilhelm Meister*, God knows—are simply those that allow the ordinary scenes they evoke to be pervaded by memories, regrets, aspirations . . . These take root in our minds much more profoundly than when eros seeks to reduce beings to its system of signs. Hence those instants, at least, when such intuitions pierce through language, open its avenues again, trace the figure of a more primal desire—more disinterested, more loving: a desire integral to us, though we don't know how to let it bloom. Moments of writing, but which signify presence. Sudden rays of sun, even at evening, under the overcast sky of our delusions. Sentences such as Goethe's about bedazzlement seem like little more than dreams; in reality, they're equally informed by a love that would free its object from the shadow of our dreams.

Something summons me in the *Wilhelm Meister* novels, and leads me to acknowledge these books—above all the second one, *The Journeyman Years*—as among the most daring breakthroughs in the quest of what we are, or what we could be.

All the same, yielding to other needs, I've noticed, I've loved—I've even copied down—other sentences. A case in point: here I have before me, on a little scrap of cardboard, often lost since the early fifties but always found again, just a few words. They refer no doubt to Federico da Montefeltro, of whom Piero della Francesca made a magnificent portrait: 'The duke cared for nothing but eternity, and the fundamental beauty of architecture.' This is another lightning flash, another momentous streak of colour above the same darkened earth . . . the rumble of visions, of energies amassed in another angle of the sky . . .

There, does an Intelligible exist, where those half-glimpses, or others still, jostle and yet align themselves perhaps into a single sentence, that of our clouds and of our thunderbolt? Is there a path, in our earthly place, that guides us on beneath this sky and towards it—even if, in this sketch where the painter left the image, we remain in the lower part, dimly lit?

Hands That Take Hold of His

He tries to write this word. But why don't the letters present themselves as they should, under his pen? After the *a*, already there's nothing more than steep bypaths, stones without end, blanched and threatening—which for all that, are maybe the letter *m*. Though further on! Years have passed, and he's still trying to form the third letter, always in vain. People surround him, they pity him, they'd like to help him . . . Ah, success at last! A large, steady hand guides his own, and now in his writing—which is still no more than birds flying quite low, in a murky rough-and-tumble—he moves on once again, his eyes closed, his feet picking their way through puddles, towards the rising sun.

Variant: He was writing a word, one of those words blocked by stones, overgrown with briars. It was silent, utterly black on the endlessly visible incline he struggled to climb.

And one day, in this word that forked, that petered out, that recommenced—a trail waxing more and more precipitous, with great disappointments, grievous sadness—one day, out of the blue, the earth sprang beneath his step, the horizon turned bright, the summits cleared, and everything (how can I put this?) was laughing. This was no longer the earlier or lower laugh in language, the one that fools itself—that jeers, hurts, destroys. This laugh was a power that welled up from the chasms on every side, from the rockface walls, from the torrents in the valley depths; their turbulence was motionless up here, in this vast meadow sloping beneath the sky—nothing more than this softness, this fresh air, these two hands taking hold of his. Childhood itself, once again, but without the anguish. Simple reality, as when the waters enfolded Empedocles, now appeased.

Zeuxis: The Self-Portrait

The vaunted portrait, which Zeuxis painted at the end of his long life, has been found again. Here it is on a picture rail, in this rear courtyard of a blighted neighbourhood. It seems Zeuxis was able to observe only a portion of his face. The left half is missing, yet this isn't an unfinished work: instead, we note something like a chasm; the painter must have peered over its edge, with a lump in his throat from vertigo. If we in turn draw close to that abyss, we see—far below the crumbling, fractured rim—some scraggly bushes growing on the cliffside, with large, sad birds devouring their berries; and still lower, eddies of colourless water.

Visitors go up to the chasm, warily look down for a bit, then move on in silence. I'm here in turn: I scrutinize the immensity, foggy in certain spots. The tomb of Zeuxis is at the bend of two mountains, on the other side of the gap. Aided by the telescope we've been offered (but which few accept), I discern that a rockslide of red stones blocks the path, so it will remain deserted forever. Only the birds painted by Zeuxis, halfway up the cliff, can fly with great beating wings to his final resting place. Then they veer back towards us; they screech in the narrow gallery and brush by us, filling us with dread.

BECKETT'S DINGHY

The island isn't far from the coast: it's a flat line hard to make out, topped by several trees, in the fog that hunkers down on the sea. All we know about the man who's taking us there in his boat is that he's kindly offered to show us around. It's raining when we push off, and we cross the narrow sound under a veil of inky shadows. We seem to be punching a hole in appearances, dreaming another world; and maybe we've almost reached it: a dim glimmer in the splotches of darkness. But after a few minutes, here's the shore. A tiny landing, where you disembark on three or four steps, hewn from glistening stone. Two little buildings, a light in one: the shut-up pub and the pub-keeper's house. He opens it on Sundays now and then, for the farmers from the other island, when they want to travel even farther west. But we don't approach the buildings; we go inland, to the right. The path is sodden—when there's a path at all—and we slog through a puddle-infested moor. We have to pick our way over barbed-wire fences—no easy feat. I scarcely understand our guide's rough, splendid accent, in a language foreign to me. Who knows where we're really headed: maybe to a stone cross from Celtic times, facing the surf; maybe just to the far side of the island. And in fact, now we've reached it. Here's the outer edge, with stout green waves in front of us; the rain has almost stopped.

We stay there for a while, at the tip of the island, admiring the ocean. We also look back at the path we've followed, or sidestepped—because of the holes, or for no reason at all. It's just a vague track that weaves through the scrubby grass, bordered here and there by low walls of stone. Then we set out on a wider trail that hugs the coast. Our guide, our friend, goes on talking. Since the surf's not as loud and the walking is easier, I understand him better now—perhaps because he's also turned to other thoughts. At any rate, tucked behind a tree, we come upon another house: so there's a third one on the island. It's only a couple of steps from the sea, but it has a small enclosure. Lettuce, parsley and potatoes used to grow there; some flowers as well, sheltered by a wedge of rock. 'Oh, the old lady who lived here!' the mariner says. He's a seaman, he just explained to us, and every year he carries a cargo around the world. 'When I was a child, she taught me in school, and later, for a long, long time, when I'd pass this way at night, I always knocked on her door. No matter if it was midnight, one or two in the morning, or almost dawn, I knew she'd be awake and dressed. She'd either be pottering around or sitting in her armchair next to the fire. And she'd open the door, laugh and serve me some tea while she told me her stories. She had tons of them.'

He reminisces, but then falls silent, as though he's listening to a voice. 'She's no longer with us,' he adds. We've circled back to the hamlet, the first pair of buildings. He insists we visit the pub. He knocks on the other door: a young woman with a child appears. He returns with the key, and jiggles it in the lock. We enter the pitch-black room, and he lights a lamp. Tables against the wall, the usual bar—though the bottles are empty, no doubt. The broad, bare floor seems worn, as though people had danced there thousands of times: in a past removed from our present, like water that's retreated far from shore. We're here to see the photographs on the wall; they're supposed to tell us about the former inhabitants of these two islands, before their community scattered and died out. Men and women dwell in another bank of fog: this paper that yellows and fades, like a metaphor of memory. Some of their faces stare back at us, distractedly reproachful, as though absorbed by a faraway vision—a knowledge, perhaps—that we can no longer share. Ireland from the forties and fifties, mysterious as a ship skirting the coast.

'And that one there, what a drinker he was!' the long-distance captain exclaims. The picture shows an old man seated in front of the ocean, pipe in hand: skinny, upright, stock-still. 'He'd cast off and catch lobsters for days on end, alone in his little dinghy. But he'd already be drunk before he left, and he'd stow flasks of whiskey with his nets and baskets. How on earth did he buck the worst of the weather and come back? Well, he always came back, so he must've been in God's own hand.'

I look at the beautiful face, which resembles Samuel Beckett's. And I forget about the alcohol: merely a device of universal writing, this hand that seeks the hand of God. I think how the writer, too, has just vanished in the distance. He's slipped away into the throng of shadows, blackened by rain or fog; though here and there—and over there again—we glimpse a streak of yellow sun. Beckett, I tell myself, wrote the way that old man sailed, alone on the sea. Like him, he spent long days and nights beneath the clouds I've watched here, piling up as castles in the sky, as cliffs, with dragons spitting fire from their ridges and crevasses. Suddenly, they shear apart before a sweeping beam, a 'spell of light', around three in the afternoon. From then until the evening swiftly falls, time slows to a halt, and gold seems to lie in the ocean's gentle hollows. Beckett is far from us now, though his boat is still dimly visible: maybe over there, where sunset ruffles a crest of sea. We should listen to his books only through the constant roll of waves, the intermittent drumming of the rain.

Another Era of Writing

I

'You see,' says my friend from over there (we're in the woods, following a narrow path with many bends; it's still morning, and there's some mist on the ground, even a bit on the branches), 'there was a time when we had quite another idea of writing, or even perhaps of language. Then, we didn't write words with these brushstrokes, which imitate so badly the thing being said; no, we noted down each one of their sounds, their phonemes . . .'

'Like us,' I tell him. I'm interested—all ears.

He smiles. 'Like you—but not as meagrely, all the same. Do you seriously feel you're still worthy of the universe, as it appears in your words? Or even more simply, worthy of your own voice—which quickens with excitement, which longs for music—when all you do is trace those downstrokes that end with black spots? My friend, we represented the sound *a*—let's say—by a jar we kept near us, in the very space where we're born and where we die. We poured water into the jar, and sometimes oil or even wine, up to different levels. From one jar to the next, other aspects also varied: the contours of the pot, the colour of the clay—not to mention the white squiggle our scribes might dab on the vase, unless they ventured to sketch an image there. Well, that was a lot of reality, as you might say, in just a letter—don't you agree? Our signs were things, and so they ended up becoming infinite. And since infinity always stays equal to itself, at least at first glance, the gap that troubles you between the sign and the thing—you regard it as arbitrary, you've taught me—was bridged, don't you think?'

'I don't know,' I tell him. 'After all, between these signs that are things and the objects they denote, the sounds of a word still persist—and they engender our dismay, our predicament. They harbour music, you say, and our excitement? But this music is ourselves—beings of illusion and death—and not that red cloud, way over there, or even just this little bud that's about to open. Look, it's ignorant of itself, at peace. Our snares start with our voice, with this all too imperfect re-creation of the world. That's where our exile already begins.'

'Yes, we can say that,' my companion sighs. 'Maybe those letters of ours made us neglect the fact that the sounds still existed: the two were so unalike! You had to have eyes to see them, but also hands to take hold of them. Sometimes you had to breathe them. Then again, you might have to walk for hours through the night on a sodden path, in order to reach one. For example—though I'm making this up—a pile of stones that could only mean a certain phoneme, thanks to the small copse of oaks and almond trees around it, beneath the sky of early morning.

'There you have it! Diametrically opposed to the abstraction that speech remains, we found a fullness of real things in our writing. Wasn't that a way of repairing, then—somewhat repairing—the wrong inflicted by words on the world? Suppose I have to write "the rose", and the chance sounds that determine our signs represent it by a glass bowl, set on a lacquer table, beside a sleeping child. The child breathes tranquilly: we're already reassured by this—maybe after several days of fever. Still, we listen to that breathing with some alarm as yet. We also know that those eyes hidden by a pillow will open, dispelling the letter that owed its existence to their sleep. What does it matter then, my friend—what does it matter from now on—if the few phonemes in the name of the rose had torn, through their sound, one of the seamless robe's thousand folds? It's mended now, or at least we can let ourselves believe so. We were dreaming the world—we're still dreaming it, perhaps—but by sleeping in it anew, among things as they are. At peace, as you were saying. Happily, don't you believe?'

We're still walking, under the trees. To the left of the path, now there's a slope, with a stream far below that leaps along the stones.

'What is happiness?' I replied.

He looked at me—attentively, or so it seemed. 'Yes. What is happiness?' he went on. 'But to tell the truth, my friend, did we ever have the time to ask ourselves that question? Think about it: reading was quite difficult, and so it was very time-consuming and absorbing, because our signs and their usages were so complex. Ah, try to understand, if you will, what one of our writings must have been like! Imagine here before you the blue glass bowl, and there, the lamp, there, the grey ceramic stove, and there, the rat in its cage. These things—that is, of course, these letters—signify something: they form a word, since they've been grouped together, along with a good many others, in this room. But in what order should they be read, scattered as they are between the window and the doors? When, and how many times, will we need to pass by one or the other, in our deciphering that now begins? The jar, the letter *a*, rests on the low table, which is *m*. But the wall behind the jar has a value as well—it's *r*—and so do we need to add it to our reading? Not forgetting that if it's joined to a floor of a reddish-ochre colour, that value is altered. If you walk around this room of words—which opens onto others, by the way—such worries will plague you, believe me. Thousands of usages have been forged from these words, in the silence that blankets them. You have to unearth those texts, re-read them—it's even urgent at times. Yet ambiguities abound, which constantly threaten to sever that airy, arachnoid thread that guides us from letter to letter, or so we'd like to think . . . Yes, often there were moments of horrible tension—you can take it from me. There were people who would burst out sobbing, who started shouting—at the fever pitch of their need, when too much anguish had mounted up. True, afterwards they seemed to lapse into lengthy spells of serenity, at least in appearance . . . It was in hours such as this that we asked ourselves questions, though quite unlike the ones we've just evoked . . .'

He broke off. 'I'm giving you a lecture, my poor traveller friend. Forgive me.'

But right away, he started up again: 'What made reading even more difficult, you see, was that while many of the things set before our eyes meant nothing, of course, we often forgot this or no longer wanted to admit it, seized by a kind of vertigo. The blue-tiled floor beneath the thin straw mat is the sound *i*, let's allow—the short *i*. But the mat itself, or the ant that chances to cross it—no, that doesn't correspond to any sound: that's nothing. Nor does the large statue aim to hint at anything, though it smiles with closed eyes near the ancestors' altar. The same applies to the sky of summer mornings—even if it's sometimes thought to denote a variant of the *u* sound (alas, there are all too many of those), when traversed by feathery clouds. Indeed, you won't be surprised that only a minor portion of our referents in the world counted for a letter, though the alphabet varied—at times rather quickly—leaving many disaffected signs in its wake. Certain scribes liked to take them up again, as an archaicizing mannerism. The number of signs was no more than that of flat stones along the path, let's say; it was nothing compared to the masses of rocks on the mountain. Still, this was a matter that troubled us and sparked our discussions—which swiftly led us to metaphysical issues.

'At the outset, all the same, we only tackled the most urgent problems, those that seemed no more than technical. How can we continue reading, if we don't know whether such-and-such an object that's caught our attention—and why, among all the others we barely register—pertains to a backcountry of the sign, forgotten today but opened up long ago? Or does it only have the value of a plain and simple thing? This partly unwound spool, its black thread trailing along the table beside the jar—in what outmoded alphabet book should we trace it down? And this lake on the horizon, filled at evening by the huge reflection of the mountains, where a red flame is dying out—will you have to forget it, through a certain choice of method? Or should you go there—if need be, for days on end—exploring its shoreline to find the blue bowl on the low lacquer table? Shouldn't it be waiting for you somewhere, as pointed out in your current reading by the sky (now and then, a sort of hyphen in our manuscripts)? Such were some of our habitual debates: believe me, we pursued a great many of this ilk. They kept us peering at a desert rose, as we passed it from hand to hand; or a reflection in the water of a basin; or even a piece of soap, which at first seemed like nothing at all, on this lid with a rusty rim.

'But quickly we ran up against further questions, and these made us leave off our readings to undertake long walks in the countryside. We talked excitedly, scrutinizing the eyes of our friends or chance companions, so as to gauge the extent of our shared disquiet. Since our writing is so unreliable, we asked ourselves at the time, shouldn't we give up the very idea of reading, at least in the former sense of that word? We could learn texts by heart, thanks to our oral traditions—those that haven't disappeared. Then we could write them, though only for ourselves from now on. Our gaze could wander along the surface of the world, could identify certain things that are signs; it could alight on them for a while, then go back to them whenever the memorized words required it. In this way, the days of our lives would be spent—and as an upshot, who knows what knowledge, or what experience, might illumine our final hours? Some people put this idea into practice. You'd observe them passing in silence; if they were approached, they had to tear themselves away from their soft-spoken writing. There can be no doubt that inscribing like this, and inscribing again, afforded a tremendous joy, almost an ecstasy. And so did reading a bit, all the same—once the memory had ascended the inscription's last meanders, only to float back down like a peaceful boat. What had prevented yesterday's scribes from being enlightened, from being delivered? they asked us. It was their fruitless worry over amassing signs in a space as confined as possible—to facilitate reading, or so they believed. Instead, let's let signs turn up at random in our existence. Through an operation of the mind, let's not hesitate to place that jar we see over there, on a farmhouse threshold, beside the stream of yesterday's walk that persists in our memory. And by the grace of mental embodiment, let's learn to retain, from the futile spectacle of the world, only those graphs that suit us. Little by little, let's separate them from it, so we can withdraw into this other space, henceforth delivered from time—since time ceases, don't you agree, wherever the sign begins?

'Some even thought that those poems from the past, conceived on far too narrow a page, weren't really needed in our current age. Why not improvise, after all, as we move among these scattered signs with a vacant stare? But that's when the heresy arose that spelt the end of an entire era. Was it because those more meditative, interior relations with great texts had restored some of its importance to that auditory dimension—between meaning and letter—we'd sought to expunge from the world? In any case, these new readers could never stop contemplating the objects they'd elected. The jar no longer sufficed for them without protracted intervals lived beside it, watching the sun enfold it with light against a plaster wall—which added nothing to the pot except its mute materiality, its naked whiteness. In this manner, letters and words were circumscribed by a plain reality of another sort. In some of them it may have effaced their phonemes' abstraction, but only by gradually detaching us from the very idea of speech. We invented painting, let's say. This took the form of brief texts—sometimes only seventeen signs—where what counted was their appearance, against a background of sky and stones, and no longer their meaning. At times the latter was consigned to wayward metaphors, or went lacking altogether. This left some among us, God knows why, with an aftertaste of sadness.

'A world was coming to an end, my friend. And that was when still others, among these honest witnesses of language in peril, took the decision, one by one, to distance themselves from society with only a few signs. Those signs relied—albeit at the expense of their primal reality—on ordinary things with which it's possible and even easy to live, without wanting more. Returning to what's simple, through employments as silent as possible, couldn't we unlearn what the letter *a* had once been— uselessly from now on—in the everyday jar? In the log that's about to burn, what had turned that instant of tiny flames and smoke into a word? By speaking needlessly of something else, that word had almost deprived us of fire. We wanted to cleanse these objects, converted into signs with some arbitrary meaning—just as the gold-digger rinses in a stream the speck he's discovered in the sand. We wanted to regain the shimmer we sense in a tree when it signifies nothing but itself . . . the light in the arm as well that reaches up, in the hand that culls the fruit.

'And that was the beginning of our notations today, which evoke the word at one go, by a stroke that no longer imitates its sounds, but the thing being said. At any rate, a good many of these seekers of simplicity seemed happy with their fate. Hermits retired to their huts, with only a jug, a bowl, a net for fishing in the water nearby. What hymns they could've composed with so few signs, or so few things, I don't know. All the same, it was said they listened to their former thoughts, freed from reveries, becoming reduced to this wicker creel, this jug brimming over with water, this bowl—and beyond that, maybe, to two or three trees, to the grass underfoot, to the path that trails off among other trees. Newlyweds and lovers felt drawn to their vicinity: as a matter of fact, this turned into a fashion. They had cottages built—of rammed earth, thatch and glass. Their life was a success when they'd reached the stage of saying nothing any more, or nothing even to themselves, except those few words—infinite, without a doubt—which offer the mind no more than the unmade bed, the fire that smokes before it catches, the griddle where chestnuts crackle, or at most, the beauty of fruits. Yes, many people back then wanted to detach themselves from those signs that had usurped the place of things. But tell me: was it possible?'

'There were methods, I suppose. The litany. Constantly repeating the name of fire . . .'

'Which could be written, in effect. According to some, it was a happenstance that boded well: fire falling from the sky on a stone, after a brief flash between two clouds. It's true there were techniques to recover plain reality, to cure it of the wound that had harmed so many things. But that's exactly it! This evil had run so deep, wouldn't the work be infinite?'

'Was it really an evil?'

'An evil, dear friend—and it ended in failure once again. The hermits died, the little cottages were left deserted. I won't recount our twilight to you, and how we abandoned our writing—all too beautiful.'

'I would've loved it,' I murmured. 'Listening to you, I felt myself growing attached to it already—though maybe I too would have been one of the hermits. Or rather, one of those who reflect on them, who hover near their clearings—like certain unbelievers, whose heart throbs more strongly when someone speaks of God.'

On an impulse, I added: 'And you? What did you think of that writing? Do you miss it, now and then?'

He burst out laughing. It was the first time.

'Miss it?' he said. 'Look, let's go inside this cabin.'

II

As it happened, we'd reached the end of that path beneath the trees. At the edge of the stream—which fanned out here on light-blue sand—a small clapboard house had just come into view. Its planks had once been painted: you could still pick out some traces of red-ochre and green. The roof was fitted with those whimsical tiles like coxcombs, often used for temples in this part of the world. But a rickety porch, interlaced by the remnants of a vine, enclosed and sheltered the threshold: and so, this was only—had always been—a place for everyday life. Since the door was hanging open, we entered the woodland abode readily enough. It was as cramped as I'd assumed— though today I believe I was wrong: that this was only one of its rooms. Neglect prevailed inside, amid the dust of withered leaves. Right away I whiffed the scent of incense, tinged with an acrid smell that betrayed a hidden mouse— confirmed by a torn sack of rice near one window. Then I saw the objects, which seemed to shed a radiance in the slight penumbra. Here, on the low, red-lacquer table: the jar. And there, and there (my gaze made them out one by one, like the stars at dusk): the lamp, the bowls, a clock, a hefty stone, the bed and so many other things. Some of them, presumably, didn't relate to writing—for example, those ashes scattered before the hearth, or this musical instrument, which I decided to call a mandora. On the other side of the table was a window, and I went up to it. I looked out over several acres of bamboo, wrested in the past from denser woods. But in front of the slender foliage, faintly ruffled by the warming light, what was that courtyard where objects had aged? Things that life's a bit ashamed of, or has left behind: a watering can, a ladder, earthen pots. Flush with the ground, patches of shadow still lingered. Higher up . . . And light? I said to myself. Here, was that just a letter among the rest, while in the West we make it the principle that transcends all words?

'Look,' murmured my companion. 'The sparkle of the noonday sun, on the rim of this porcelain bowl.'

And he added: 'This house where we are is "Forgotten Woods" . . . a famous poem back then, presented here in a so-called poor edition. There was a time, not so long ago, when many of us knew that all the sounds of those fourteen remarkable verses could be derived from these objects, linked by an invisible thread. But it was also a time when some of our lettered people started finding an inherent virtue in their meaning, a particular strength where they placed all their hope. The author, they told themselves, had obviously loved existence as it used to flow from life in former days—water that widens on the sand, in the light. Because of this, he'd learnt to disavow the lure of dreams: he wouldn't have valued those crystals of make-believe—bizarre at times, or even perverse— which our alphabet deposits in the praxis of the world. Accordingly, would he have permitted his faithful readers—those who would re-decipher him on and on, who through his phrases would forget all human discourse, sullied elsewhere by dreams—to watch their signs ineluctably fade away? Fade away in regard to the objects, the places, the situations in their lives? Those signs we've forged with such recklessness on the whole, abetted by things? A text from the past, my friend, so as to unlearn the very writing that conveyed it—a text that would allow us to foil the entrapment where we'd been caught, by wanting to conserve it; a text to recover the voice alone, the voice at peace with these phonemes, these sounds.

Maybe they don't arise from our excessiveness after all, from our arrogant abstraction, but are simply the most minimal gap we could conceive, apart from predation, between the mind and the world . . .

'I won't expound to you, my dear companion, the philosophy of language you'll detect being formulated here. For that matter, have I really understood it? Back then, in those woods where thought took refuge as the century waned, it was more or less agreed that the human voice is like a Pan's flute: an almost natural instrument, a breath where the body is gathered up—and with it, all of nature. From that perspective, there's nothing arbitrary about phonemes in themselves. Far more than a reflection of what is, they would comprise a part of it, closely linked through correspondences with many elements of the thing being said. It was also affirmed that if the word "night" seems luminous, while night is dark, this doesn't matter much in the end. Don't we also lose our way in the actual woods? Through its own thickets, language can relive quite well the stumbling blocks of the real, where we meet with hardships—but consequently, also with our truth. As you'll note, no one worried any more about the contingency of signifiers in those years when a world was falling apart.

'And so we repeated this poem, about a deceased woman who can come to life again—forgetting the heavy, useless flowers piled upon her body—if only someone will murmur her name with love, throughout an entire evening . . . Was that the way forward? The passage beyond our signs with their numerous traps, the secret so many of us had sought—as I was telling you? I remember the visits to this wooden house, or to other modest dwellings that proposed the same poem. You came alone, because it speaks of absence. Or with someone else, because it speaks of love. Often you had to travel a long time, your knees quaking with fatigue. You entered with respect, you read a little . . . it was only the first day. After that you slept, while the light was changing. Beautiful days now began, amid the rustling of airy branches and shadows. You had slept, then: among the things around you, sleep still retained its puddles of water, almost black. But quickly you took hold of the earthen pot, you cooked some rice and had something to eat. Or else you wanted to stay in bed a while longer, and left the door shut—at times until evening, when the young woman went out to wash the bowls in the clear-running stream.'

'You lived here,' I said abruptly. (I was smiling—but mainly because I was moved. My voice caught a little in my throat.)

'Yes,' he told me.

'But you didn't stay?'

My friend didn't answer right away.

'Of course,' he replied at last. 'I had come here alone. And I'd also come without knowing any sorrow, contrary to what the poem supposes, or even requires. Why did I want this poem instead of another? (A few had been suggested, in the forest.) I even asked myself that question, however fleetingly. Had I chosen badly? Or had I been wrong to believe I needed such choices? In any case, from the outset, it wasn't what I'd expected. The poem I loved and knew by heart was certainly here: silent, in the nexus of almost discernible links that bound the signs together. In the extinguished fireplace or the clock, I could sense its light filtering through. In the rekindled hearth, it led me to hear no more than the fire's sound; or in the tilted jar, the sound of water filling a glass. But this is precisely when my thoughts went astray. Not that I felt summoned once again by the strange, stellar outline made by the jar and the lamp and this mandora, side by side—in God knows what night of the mind. The sign that was the thing lay well shrouded in mist, as it must—but did this happen in the wished-for way? Let's say it was the objects themselves that withdrew so deeply into their form, emptied of any meaning from now on, that they were no longer signs for me—yet nothing of this world, either. In other words, the clock's ticking no longer expressed that it was the clock: no, the tick-tock had detached itself from the idea of telling time. And when midnight struck its twelve strokes, that pointless number—as the poet asked us to regard it— well, I didn't even count them any more. All too overtly, the sound issued from an abyss, and that's where I heard it sink away again. I could tell you the same of the fire I kept unlit, even if its flame was a letter; the same of the chair beside the fire; the same of the mirror—though admittedly, its place in our writing has always been con- tested, always a subject of unease.

'And soon, my friend, I reached the stage of struggling to form any words, I felt so distracted by each object: by what within it went beyond its status as a sign, yet also dispelled its first identity—which I'd believed to be inviol- able. I turned towards the enigmatic clock, plunged for long spells in staring at its polished wood, black with a reddish grain. I frequently returned to the windowsill (not without effort; still, this was an obligation, since there a word implied by the poem takes shape). All I could register any more was the ants that often mill there, helter-skelter. It's fascinating, to be sure: they crisscross in a jumble. One ant rushes to what might be an intersection where others balk: at times the melee seems to comprise a sign again— but clearly, of another nature. Could I call it figurative? Obviously, it meant no more than the patterns of foam along a shore, when the waves recede—infinite though they are. I was drawn as well to a nail on the wall, which stuck out a bit. Every time I should've fixed on a word, or recomposed a verse, my gaze would circle back to that nail. I wasn't wondering if it was yet another sign, as I've told you we constantly did—among so many graphs nearly forgotten, and in the wake of so many scribes. No, it was simply because it had skewed when it pierced the wood: and so this nub of iron appeared more real, from then on, than everything that looms and roils in our minds. That nail was the centre of the world. Or rather, it was the rock where every idea of the world came to break. I might even say: *it was*. And also, dreadfully: *it was not*.

'After this, one day I went out in the evening, as I'd often done; but on that night the moon was full. The whole forest was visible: in the faint shadows, where a chilly wind was blowing, I could distinguish all the trees, all the stones. It dawned on me that each of them had precise contours, endowed with an infinite number of features: while form means nothing, it assures to each of them what we might call its being, in the solitude of those dells and high plateaus beneath the moon. This is harrowing, don't you think? A wolf was howling in the distance, intent on its hunt or its dream. The stream was plashing, just as it is now—but maybe somewhat louder, since it had rained a lot several days before. And all of a sudden, an idea shot through me, like the thunderbolt gone missing from this motionless world.

'What blindness!' I said to myself at first. (While everything became clear to me in a flash, there were various planes to my intuition; I passed through each of them in turn.) 'Our writing is like an eye bereft of a gaze! It doesn't differentiate between the table and lamp I see here (or even the sleeping child), and other tables and lamps in other places, in other lives. Of course, our writing assumes it has discerned the infinite facets of an object it's converted into a letter: that's even why it claims to retrieve the infinity in the initial thing said, despite the word's abstraction. But for this very reason, our writing doesn't know what allows us to say, "Here, you see, is a tree," without focusing on this tree right before us—with the marks peculiar to it, its unique relation to a place, the line of its crown that's unlike any other. And so, our writing sacrifices once again the fact of existing here, in this moment, to the evocation of an essence: which dooms the thing it names to be perceived—it, too—as nothing more than an idea, an absence. We've only condensed the sign, without triumphing over its fault. However much we raise or lower the water in the lovely jar, we'll have done no more than calligraph the sign instead of ripping it apart, sending up a cry. Don't you agree?'

'You're contradicting yourself,' I remarked. 'A while ago, you talked of the peaceful impression instilled by the child we watch sleeping, near the table and the glass.'

'We were dreaming, as I told you. We were imagining what doesn't exist. And meanwhile . . . Look, here it is,' he added.

As he was speaking, in fact, my friend had walked across the room, and now he showed me the nail he'd mentioned, on the wall near the window. It was a chunk of black iron, fairly rusty; it had been hammered into the blue-painted wood somewhat crookedly, though not too much. My companion peered at the nail for several moments, in silence. The exaltation that had swept over him seemed to abate.

'We were dreaming,' he resumed. 'And the price of dreaming is the void to which we condemn all things.

'You're going to tell me,' he continued, staring at me with a certain insistence, 'that all I'd done was discover for myself what the poem sets forth, when it evokes a death and a resurrection—that I was only encountering what others besides myself were seeking and finding in its words, when they would come to this house. They were better suited to understand, since soon they would con-clude that these few objects sufficed for a life. They would engage in that daily companionship with them that trans-forms everything around us into an absolute, as they say. But I didn't reason that way!

'Because' (and he stood erect at these words; he seemed to grow taller; his eyes glowed) 'what I discovered in that very moment beneath the sky, among the trees and stones, near the elusive animals, is that whatever intimacy we may enjoy with several objects we like is nothing. It's only a mirage again, that absolute: since there's still all the rest! Let's set aside those signs—which may never have existed, which may only have been my delusion. Imagine those you love, those of whom you're fond, and how you dream that they might *be*—absolutely and eternally, as on a pillar of fire rising from the abyss. Well then, in order for them to exist like that, above the abyss, doesn't everything else have to exist as well? Tell me, are we, if the woodpecker over there, pecking on the tree trunk—you hear him, don't you—is not? If in the sea, there's a single drop of nothingness? If in the sand of the beaches, there's a single grain that is not?'

'The sand isn't self-aware,' I ventured to say.

'It's self-aware through me when I scoop it up, when I let it sift through my hands, when I look at it. And it follows that I'm responsible for it! Yes, in that moment, you see, I felt a wave of responsibility—which crushed me.'

He fell silent. I wished I could unravel his madness, assuage his suffering—but nothing occurred to me. He went on:

'In any case, that was only the initial plane, as I've told you. Already I saw the great thought taking shape in me, the thunderbolt that taught me salvation. I was in the woods, then—but on paths whose luminous ground was like that other shore, stretching across the sky. First off, I beheld at a single glance the number of beings and of things. Then I told myself that each being and each thing, unique as they were, all of them, in the abyss where their difference shines out—yes, what singles out this ant from that one, this stone from that one—were in that very difference, by it and by the grace of it, the signifier of a sound. Each was the emblem—arbitrary, to be sure—of a phoneme, as you say, in the notation of a language that would have, by that token, as many phonemes as there are stars in the sky, and atoms in those stars. I conceived that by using these numberless phonemes just as we do in our everyday speech, unnumbered thousands of times for even the rarest among them, this language would be capable—not of an infinity of types of phrases, like ours—but of much more, infinitely more: of an infinity of infinites instead of merely one, if I may put it that way. I finally grasped that only a god, with his infinite number of mouths, could speak this language, and that only he could write it. And then, by gauging the lie of writing just like us, rebounding athwart it to the experience of being, only he could fix and found in words that being which for us always escapes them. Only he could grant that being to this sad world—this time around as it should be, with all creatures and all things benefitting from its breath, happily together as one . . . I understood this, I saw it. I had proved the existence of God by the infinite number of things, by their usage as signs, by the critique of those signs—and I could see him swimming now in this foam of worlds, approaching a shore. I was raving mad, no doubt you'll say?'

'You were simply becoming one of ours,' I answered, without any pride.

'I went back in, at any rate; but from now on, I knew that for me it was over—this house in the woods, these objects, this idyll of peace and self-satisfaction others believed they were pursuing here. True, I stayed on for several more days—mulling over my memories, perhaps. Then I departed, not touching a thing. I even left the celebrant in its place on the wall . . .'

'The celebrant?'

'That was the name we gave to those rusty nails.'

'They were known, then?'

'We called them that, anyway. But without stating their use.'

'You should've remained several days more. As for me, I'd have liked to live near this celebrant, since that's what it's called.'

He smiled. 'You couldn't have,' he told me. Then he added: 'You'll forget it.' After that, he took from my hands a bundle I'd found on the table, a sheaf of pages barred with words. He headed for the hearth. Leaning down, he gathered a few of the branches with dry leaves strewn across the floor—I hadn't noticed them till now, though there were many. He tore up the paper, scattering it on top of them. Soon the fire was built; it burned high and bright. We went out.

Night had fallen now. We could make out some stars. With my guide (since I can't call him my master), I walked away. But after several steps, I turned around: for one more moment, I wanted to look at this place again, where I was leaving so much of myself behind.

In fact, I caught sight of the house—despite the bend in the path, despite the crowded trees. The tiles of the roof, those coxcombs now gone black, stood out against the sky where the moon was riding, among the clouds. And through that door that couldn't be closed, across the threshold where a sudden, powerful wind was rushing in as it shook the trees, I saw that the firelight had grown, that it was burning brighter and brighter—that it was dancing in the entire room.

Bonnefoy the Voyager:
A Translator's Afterword

'One day,' said Yves Bonnefoy in October 1969, 'they'll ask you to write a thesis. As a topic, I'd suggest "Baudelaire et le voyage"—later, you could expand that essay into a book.' We were sitting in his library on rue Lepic, a steep, winding street in Montmartre. I was only nineteen, and so a thesis—much less a book—seemed remote, though I did like the subject he had proposed. Nine years down the line, also at his incentive, I would finish my Oxford dissertation in a different field altogether: late-Renaissance poetics. Even so, that Baudelairean afternoon is forever lodged in my memory. In his measured voice, Bonnefoy read aloud 'Le voyage', followed by 'L'Invitation au voyage'. He then commented drolly that in the main Baudelaire was a virtual traveller, not a practitioner—rather like the hapless albatross of his emblematic poem. Tormented, irresolute— except in the decisive domains of metre and form—

Baudelaire would watch the coveted haven of 'luxe, calme et volupté' recede from his grasp. His two excursions, to Réunion in his youth and to Belgium in his final months, both ended in frustration and disillusionment. Paris would remain the prime arena of his existence—a 'city that changes its shape,' he mused with regret, 'more quickly than a mortal's heart.'

By contrast, Bonnefoy was an ardent voyager throughout his life. His constant journeys and sojourns abroad left an obvious imprint on his oeuvre. We need only think of the enormous role of Italy—from his essays on the tombs of Ravenna, on Quattrocento painting, or on the Roman Baroque, to the manifold traces of Italian art and architecture in his poetry. The 'land of Shakespeare', as he fondly called England, also springs to mind, especially through his many translations of Shakespeare and other English-language authors. Among them was Yeats: in recognition of his superb French versions, Bonnefoy was welcomed to Sligo in 1987 as Poet in Residence. His extensive periods at universities in the United States, above all in Massachusetts and New York, influenced his writings in demonstrable ways. Within Europe, he taught in Switzerland, visited Sweden and Austria and often spent time in Germany. Much farther afield, he joined the Mexican poet Octavio Paz in India, perhaps his most ambitious voyage. Nor should we forget that for Bonnefoy, raised in the Lot Valley and the Touraine, Paris was not a native ground at all, though he lectured there for many years. Along with his early haunts, other regions in France—such as the divergent landscapes of Normandy and Provence—recur insistently in his poems.

Given Bonnefoy's continual displacements, it seems fitting that he entitled one of his major works *La Vie errante* (1993). To celebrate the centenary of his birth, *The Wandering Life* now appears in translation at Seagull Books, along with its shorter companion piece, *Une autre époque de l'écriture* (*Another Era of Writing*). Often overlooked in the past, both are paramount to the author's development. The longer book not only crystallizes the voyager theme, but also founds a new aesthetic: that symphonic interweaving of verse and prose which marks the final twenty-five years of his creation. *Another Era of Writing* employs the travel motif to stage a gripping debate on the nature of language, a central issue in Bonnefoy's lifework.

In verse, *The Wandering Life* regales us with the incantatory rhythms of 'Impressions at Sunset'. The grandiose skyscape reminds us that photographing clouds was one of the poet's favourite pastimes in the late eighties and early nineties, when he was composing *La Vie errante*. The painter, the temple-like portico, the golden god, the musicians, the twittering birds and the glowing ember give voice to multiple strands of the book's polyphony. At the opposite extreme, the laconic lines of 'A Stone' belong to a recurring sequence of lapidary poems under that title, spanning five decades of his oeuvre. Here, meaning is hollowed out, as an undue attachment to images reduces a beloved landscape to ash: a warning to any voyager that facile symbols can never supplant the immanence of the real (one rendering of 'évidence', Bonnefoy's shibboleth). The 'wandering life' is epitomized by the longest verse-cycle in the tapestry; 'From Wind and Smoke' plays obliquely on the legends sung by Homer. While Odysseus himself—prominent in other collections, such as *Les Planches courbes* (*The Curved Planks*) of 2001—is absent here, the seafaring topos is evinced by Helen's abduction to Troy, and classical islands seem to glide past us along the way. Her association with paintings or sculpted stone echoes the artistic motifs of the preceding poems in prose, an adroit example of Bonnefoy's orchestral technique; in many of these brief lyric paragraphs, such as the ones about Zeuxis or 'Glaucus the God', Greek prototypes also prevail. That Glaucus was the patron of sailors adds a further layer to the travel theme. In other passages, *The Wandering Life* expands our poetic horizons beyond the Mediterranean to hinterlands as mysterious—for a Frenchman, at least—as the esoteric depths of Iowa.

Like musical variations, the prose poems in *The Wandering Life* transpose the voyager leitmotiv across an astonishing array of tempi, dynamics and keys. In 'Read the Book!'—which stands as a prelude to the entire work—Bonnefoy revisits the garden and sideroom of one of his childhood houses. In *The Curved Planks*, he will summon it up again in a twelve-poem cycle, 'La Maison natale' ('The House Where I Was Born'). By juxtaposing that early locale with orange-trees, white sands and passengers disembarking from a ship, 'Read the Book!' depicts his voyages as at once near and far, domestic and exotic. The succeeding poems often divide these two poles into separate groups. Distant lands beckon in lines about Strabo the geographer, at the confines of the ancient world, or Ossendowski, in a snow-covered forest of Siberia. America and Western Europe also receive their due, from Chicago to Boston, and from Seville to an island off the Irish coast, where he was transported by a garrulous captain in his dinghy. (I can vouch for the 'verism' of that trip, since I met the mariner myself.) On another occasion, we amble with the poet past what seem to be the reddish cliffs of the Var in southern France; meanwhile, his thoughts foreshadow the linguistic meditations of *Another Era of Writing*. We can almost look over his shoulder as he trundles through the American Midwest in a long-range bus, reminiscing about a trancelike Indian film, a de Kooning exhibition in New York or details from canvases of the Flight into Egypt. In a cheery though undetermined spot, he attends a house party with some friends, only to be overwhelmed by the keen specificity of time and place.

Unlike the poems just cited, ostensibly anchored in everyday experience, many of the prose pieces in *The Wandering Life* adhere to a genre invented by Bonnefoy: he christened such stories 'récits en rêve', or 'tales within dreams'. Even if they begin in a down-to-earth mode, they soon take on an oneiric flair, not unlike the fictions of

Jorge Luis Borges. True to the voyager theme, in 'All Morning in the City' the narrator sets out with his guidebook to explore a splendid metropolis. While it mirrors the Genoa Bonnefoy will describe in a much later work, 'Les Deux scènes' ('Two Stages'), here the ocean is metamorphosed into a boundless river. In a labyrinthine stroll, childhood memories mingle with novel discoveries in an alien land, so that the adventurer's inner and outer worlds intertwine. More manifestly a dream, 'Two Musicians, Three Perhaps' chronicles a voyage of a similar kind, to another town with a far-off shore whose inhabitants behave disconcertingly. Many of the shorter poems in the book obey a comparable pattern. And yet beyond real-life travel or wayfaring reveries, these whimsical minstrels signal another trend. The artists of every stripe who people *The Wandering Life* attest that its essential journey is an aesthetic quest.

The protagonist of 'The Alchemist of Colour' fixes his sights on an impracticable goal, the transmutation of brushstrokes into optical light. Ultimately, he achieves something far more comprehensive: landscape painting, an art that embraces the entire globe. This is underlined by the advent of the 'angels of the Earth' at the conclusion of the tale, close kindred of the 'ange de la terre' in Bonnefoy's earlier book, *Pierre écrite* (*Written Stone*), published in 1965. In *The Wandering Life*, they also double as the Theological Virtues, and the 'essential terms' that resolve a Western enigma he parses in 'Huge Red Rocks'. Their raiment in vibrant hues recalls the seraphs of Piero della Francesca—as well as Bonnefoy's pilgrimages to admire his work, not only at the Brera or Sansepulcro Museums, but also at less obvious venues such as the Clark Institute. As the poet sums up in 'All the Gold in the World', our consciousness hovers between a drifting illusionism and the plain 'thereness' before our eyes.

Art in the larger sense—not only painting and sculpture, but also architecture, music, film, fiction or poetry—should mediate between those two dimensions, conflating them into a fundamental unity. But does art truly accomplish that, or does its 'alchemy' betray simple reality with its insidious Midas touch? This is the quandary Bonnefoy approaches from myriad angles in the three cycles of verbal microcosms that follow. Paradoxically, they are devoted to Zeuxis, the acclaimed exponent of pictorial 'realism' in fifth century Greece, though they read like miniature 'tales within dreams'. The underlying dilemma is that no matter how closely an artist cleaves to nature, he still produces a mere simulacrum. As in the succinct verses of 'A Stone', representation divorces us from straightforward apprehension: if we yield to its seductive lure, if we prize the image over the actual world, our words will turn to ash. 'Our words', Bonnefoy stresses, because everything he perceives within the visual arts also applies to literature, whether we engage in it as readers ('Two Sentences, and Others') or as writers ('Hands That Take Hold of His'): at bottom, both words and images are signs.

This theme is poignantly expounded in *Another Era of Writing*, the lengthiest of the 'tales within dreams' in Bonnefoy's protean oeuvre. Tellingly, he couples it with *The Wandering Life* as an interdependent diptych: while shorter in pages, the story wields an equal heft. Set in a faraway land—like many of the vignettes in the larger book—it portrays the aesthetic path as verging on a perilous brink, the demise of language itself. When I first met Bonnefoy in 1969, he grounded me in Saussurean semiotics as a preface to his weekly tutorials on poetry. Throughout his life—as his essays reflect—he was deeply troubled by the gap between the signifier and the signified, and what that disconnection might portend for our stance towards the world. He cautioned that words, allied to concepts, inevitably drive a wedge between our minds and our surroundings. In *Another Era of Writing*, he dramatizes that existential malaise as a tense parley between two personae, both of them inherent to his own sensibility. On the one hand, we have the unquiet 'foreigner', obsessed with the disjunction of materiality and human speech; we encounter him somewhere in East Asia—as suggested by brushstroke calligraphy, ideograms based on pictures, seventeen-unit tankas, coxcomb-tiled temples and a carefully tended stand of bamboo. On the other hand, we have the narrator, self-avowedly Western, who is visiting his friend in that mythical realm. Trenchantly, we meet the 'foreigner' in his own native place, which underlines the conflation here of the narrator with his alter ego, as well as his alienation from that other self. Monopolizing the dialogue, the foreigner becomes a narrator, too, just as the narrator is also a foreigner in this country they briefly share: the kingdom of words. Listening to the foreigner's vivid account, the narrator realizes that a strange linguistic angst has plunged him into vertigo; the crisis has undermined his culture as a whole, and precipitated its decline. Ironically, by reifying the written word, by fusing phonemes and things, he and his compatriots have divorced themselves even more radically from the physical universe. The colloquy with the foreigner, wryly distanced as a 'native outlander', permits the narrator to diagnose more objectively—perhaps even to exorcize—a malady he suspects that he harbours within himself.

Despite the gravity of the interchange, Bonnefoy sometimes strikes a sardonic note. In passing, he alludes to 'the name of the rose', the title of Umberto Eco's semiotic novel about a medieval monastery; or to the trendy newlyweds who retreat to spartan cottages close to anchorites; or to the adoption of the priestly term 'celebrant' for a rusty nail on the wall. These gentle sideswipes also betoken a religious subtext that peeks in and out of the story, without becoming overly precise. At various points, we run across words like 'salvation' with a redemptive tinge, or 'light' as the highest expression of the spirit, or self-denying 'hermits' who withdraw from worldly pursuits. We even find two mentions of God with an uppercase G: one by the narrator, speaking of those who're stirred by others talking of God; and one by the foreigner, when he intones his ultimate ecstasy—an explicit vision of God. It calls to mind the 'cosmic rapture', so to speak, in 'The

his speculations. During that debate, Socrates begins by positing an organic connection between the names we give to things and their external traits; but soon he's forced to admit that correlations of this ilk can't be uniformly ascertained. Undaunted, Mallarmé dusts off the notion of a link between a signifier's phonemes and the outer facets of the signified. In his exchange, Bonnefoy echoes the fanciful complaint from the *Divagations* (already evoked in 'Read the Book!') that while 'nuit' seems light in hue, 'jour' seems dark—though pointedly, he consigns this quibble to the deluded foreigner. In other works, such as *Les Mots anglais*, Mallarmé toys with the reification of words, much like the sound-objects that spell out a system of writing in Bonnefoy's tale. Equally notable are borrowings from *Igitur*, which likens creation to a castle. The phantasmal author descends a stair to the tombs of his ancestors, presumably the founders of language. The poetic process advances through an architecture of time; at the stroke of midnight, the rite of composition will be fulfilled. In Bonnefoy's story as well, we find the clock with its twelve chimes, even if they aren't heeded: their futility is foreshadowed by 'The Clock' in *The Wandering Life*— merely a motionless, painted dial, a mocking image of eternity. In *Another Era of Writing*, Mallarmé's chateau shrinks to a cottage, though its far more rustic features also embody a poem. On a table inside it, sheets of paper are 'barred' with words—an ambivalent verb that seems to denote both lines of script and their crossing-out, their negation. As in Mallarmé's *Un Coup de dès*, the dice-throw of poesis can never 'abolish' the disorder of the universe.

This admixture of Mallarméan topoi in Bonnefoy's story should prevent us from taking the foreigner's rhapsody on God at face value, much less his claim that an infinity of signs demonstrates the godhead's existence. Instead, his vaunted deity seems more like a Deus ex machina with a capital D, conjured to reunite the cosmos with human speech. Throughout Bonnefoy's oeuvre, closing the breach between words and the real is the task he attributes not to a god but to the integrative power of poetry. His conviction that this verbal 'alchemy' should be a collective endeavour accounts in part for the many translations he authored. In 'From Wind and Smoke', he equates his originals with translations, since literature always seeks to transpose the core of being into words. His faith in that shared vocation also explains the assistance he granted to the translators of his works, into scores of different tongues. That worldwide community was not unlike a modest avatar of the polyglot numen in

Another Era of Writing. He enjoined his readers to commit themselves to the poetic act, an act he identified with hope. Yet he was also aware of the poem's evanescence, and here the 'outlander' within him resolutely challenges the narrator's Western tropes. Though the woodland cottage fleshes out fourteen cherished verses, that verbal shrine will not endure forever, like the 'marble monument' of Shakespeare's sonnet—nor will the beloved return to life through the medium of art, as in Bonnefoy's favourite play, *The Winter's Tale.* In the foreigner's poem, the deceased will magically revive if her 'name of the rose' is murmured through the night. But he concludes that no litany can resurrect our past from its flower-laden grave: in the end, he dooms both his scribbled pages and the structure around them to burn to ash. As in the 'Fire Sermon' sutra, our desires are merely flames that dwindle to nothing—like the incinerated words of 'A Stone', the monitory verses at the crux of *The Wandering Life.*

With the utmost humility, in closing I feel obliged to record a curious coincidence—though mutatis mutandis, it may also hint at the inner sources of translation, which Bonnefoy often called 'the highest form of friendship'. A year or two before he composed *Another Era of Writing,* I told him about a refuge I was building in a lonely grove of palms, not far from a clear-running stream. Roofed with tiered green tiles, it somewhat resembled a pagoda. The cabin was intended as a memorial to a friend who had died in the prime of life, and with whom I had hiked to that place. Nearly a decade after the publication of Bonnefoy's tale, I was passing through Paris, and he asked me to join him in his library on rue Lepic. 'I use this study less and less often,' he remarked, once we'd settled into our usual chairs. 'You're such an avid traveller—the Arctic, the Antarctic, Asia, Africa, South America—I never know when you'll turn up in France. I thought you might enjoy meeting me in this room again, where we started our conversations long ago.' When I mentioned I'd been translating some of his latest poems, he surprised me by replying: 'No, the text for you is *Une autre époque de l'écriture*, along with *La Vie errante*.' It was the first time he'd ever urged me to translate a specific book of his; but at that point, I was wholly absorbed in his recent verse.

Threading my way step by step through *The Wandering Life* and its corollary work, I've often had the sensation of coming full circle. I've remembered our initial discussion of the traveller motif, when Bonnefoy broached the theme of 'Baudelaire the Voyager'. During his final months, he bequeathed a 'literary legacy' to his translators, and the present book is the last of three he assigned to me. I was roaming through Southeast Asia in the weeks prior to his death, which came to pass on the day of my arrival in Europe. In our 'community of translators', we all acknowledged that given his poor state of health, our trusted friend's deliverance could only be a relief to him. Still, for me it was especially sad: I had longed to speak with him one more time—though destiny decided otherwise. From the Cambodian countryside, not unlike the backdrop of *Another Era of Writing*, I sent him a final message about the ruined smiles of Buddhas, Hindu deities and ancient kings, peacefully merging with nature once again. As to my cabin in the 'forgotten woods', it was shattered by a hurricane and swept away. Whether water and wind, or wind and fire, the elements always destroy our house of signs; but this is as it must be—since only then do we know it is 'the real that we confront'.

Hoyt Rogers
Las Siguas, 2023

Translator's Acknowledgements

I am deeply grateful to my late friend and mentor, Yves Bonnefoy, for entrusting me with this project, and to the editors at Seagull Books for bringing it to fruition. I also owe a permanent debt of appreciation to my generous colleagues, John Naughton, Stephen Romer and Anthony Rudolf. This English translation and the translator's afterword are dedicated to Grant Geiger, in memoriam.

A number of the translations in this book were included in two anthologies of Yves Bonnefoy's work: *Second Simplicity* (New Haven, CT: Yale University Press, 2012) and *Poems* (Manchester: Carcanet Press, 2018). Others first figured in the pages of *The Fortnightly Review*, *Plume Poetry*, *Mayday*, *Offcourse*, the *Apple Valley Review*, *New American Writing*, *The Southern Review*, and *Interpret*. My sincere thanks to the editors of these publications for supporting my efforts over the years.

A few more notes are in order. I borrowed the final phrase in the afterword from a poem by George Oppen. A bibliography of works by Yves Bonnefoy in English may be found in *Second Simplicity*. A supplemental list appears at the end of *Rome, 1630* (London: Seagull Books, 2020).